It Ain't Rock & Roll
The biography of drummer John Kerrison

Robin E. Hill

ISBN: 978-1-326-62208-4

PublishNation
www.publishnation.co.uk

This book is dedicated to my wonderful parents Ernest and Clare Kerrison. They were always there for me.
(John Kerrison)

Note

This biography relies heavily on John's memory and the anecdotal recollections of others, please forgive any inaccuracies. Furthermore it is impossible to consistently apply a politically correct nomenclature that would meet the approval of all points of view on the subject of disability. Additional apologies are offered to anyone who is offended by any of the terms employed in this memoir.

Angel Falls

It ain't Rock & Roll, but the hangover's still the same
Where he sits now there ain't no one else that he can blame
Luck took him down from high ground once again
He's alone in the desert, alone with no friends
It ain't Rock & Roll but the hangover's still the same
No, it ain't Rock & Roll but the hangover's still the same

CONTENTS

Part I - The Accident

Chapter One

Right from when I was twelve years old, all that I ever really wanted to do was to play the drums... I would do whatever it took to make it happen. (John Kerrison)

The light blue Volga four-door saloon gleaming in the May sunshine on that life-changing Monday morning in 1971 was John Kerrison's pride and joy. Manufactured behind the Iron Curtain, the Volga's head turning vulgar (sic) chrome trimmed design owed a great deal to the extravagant American limousines of the 1950s and 1960s. It was built like a tank with bench seats, a column gear change and a powerful engine. Underneath the car all of the suspension springs were wrapped in leather and liberally covered in grease to provide protection against the harsh Soviet winters. The rare right-hand drive variant of the prestigious vehicle had originally been supplied to the Russian Embassy in London and, several less authoritarian owners later, John had purchased it for a bargain seventy-five pounds.

It was an unusual car for a twenty-three year old working class lad from Hayes in West London to own, but it was also quite functional. The Volga provided John with transport to his work as a self-employed joiner, and the spacious interior was large enough to take a full drum kit. The latter feature was quite important because he also played the drums in a band called "The Beachcombers", a position formerly held by his friend and fellow drummer Keith "The Loon" Moon, before he began smashing drum kits and trashing hotel rooms with "The Who". John would have preferred to be on tour with a Rock & Roll band, but for the time being he had to be content

1

with performing just two or three gigs a week as a semi-professional musician. It was a situation dictated eighteen months previously when he had married northern lass Linda and then gone through the legal process to adopt her toddler son Simon. The extra responsibility of having a family to support required a steady income.

The Volga also went some way to make a statement that John was still somehow different, an anti-establishment Rock & Roll rebel, despite his current role as husband and father. It was the ideal car for a self-confessed arrogant, loudmouth, extrovert drummer who, on the Monday in question, was dressed for work in an American red checked cotton shirt with a buttoned down collar, shocking pink Levi corduroy straight legged jeans plus a pair of cherry red Dr. Martens boots. The former scooter riding Mod still managed to stand out from the crowd even in the era of flamboyant flower power hippy fashion, and particularly when wearing pink jeans on a building site. A Russian limousine was also an unusual sight on the streets of West London. People would point at the Volga and ask, "What the hell is that?" as it drove past them travelling, more often than not, at a reckless tyre screeching speed. However, on that life-changing Monday morning in May 1971, the car stubbornly refused to start and John never got the chance to drive it again.

The car had worked well enough over the previous weekend when, on Saturday evening, John had taken his wife Linda out for a meal. She hated being left at home when he was out drumming at gigs and the night out was intended as a compensatory gesture, an attempt to pour oil on the stormy waters of their tempestuous relationship.

However, the Italian restaurant was mostly John's choice of cuisine. He had become fascinated by all things *molto Italiano* when, as an impressionable teenager, he had performed with a British band at a club in Rome.

From time to time Linda did get to see her husband play the drums with The Beachcombers, but that was only when a babysitter was available. Her patience was often stretched to its limits when John returned home after a gig because, like many other professional Rock musicians, it took him quite some time to relax after the euphoric high induced by playing in front of a large audience. It is an aspect of the music business that has wrecked many marriages.

When you come home from a gig you are as high as a kite and you do not want to go to bed... a lot of musicians struggle with their wives who do not understand that. I used to get home after I had played with the band and just sit there, trying to wind down before I went to bed. (John Kerrison)

When John was just a young schoolboy he had taken drum lessons with Jim Marshall, the famous amplifier designer, before turning professional at the surprisingly young age of thirteen. He had gone on to build an impressive CV for himself as a drummer having played with various top flight bands at major venues in England, Scotland, Germany and Italy. During that time he also drummed on a number of tracks released as singles (including one recorded in Italy), performed on programmes transmitted on BBC Radio and appeared on early versions of pop videos for the UK ITV channel and German television. Several of his former associates that he had performed alongside had become international superstars in bands such as "The Tremeloes" and "Deep Purple". John had spent a decade developing his talent and learning his stagecraft. It could be said that he had completed two on-the-job apprenticeships, one as a drummer and the other as a carpenter.

On Sunday afternoon John had driven to a gig near Heathrow Airport but this time it was not with The Beachcombers, it was a rehearsal with another group of musicians. The line-up included vocalist Alan Barratt from the West London band "Jo Jo Gunne" and guitarist George Williams (who was later in the third version of "The Love Affair"). At that point they had not decided on a name for the band but there was already promising talk of a recording contract. John sensed that this could be his big chance for fame and fortune. One of the songs that the group rehearsed was "The Letter" which had been a hit for Memphis band "The Box Tops". John had not mentioned the Sunday practise session to his colleagues in The Beachcombers and he felt somewhat guilty about his disloyalty, especially towards his fellow band member and close friend Norman Mitchener. However, on the Monday morning following the rehearsal he had a more pressing problem when his car refused to start.

I don't really know why my car wouldn't start... I didn't even lift the bonnet... I don't do stuff like that. (John Kerrison)

At that time John was working on a building site at Maxwell Road in Northwood with his fellow joiner Terry Short; coincidentally, Terry's house in Hillingdon was about forty metres from where John currently lives today. When John caught the bus to his workmate's home looking for a lift to work, he found that Terry had already left and so he took another bus ride to Northwood. Fortunately, he needed only a few tools including a pump action "Yankee" screwdriver and a spirit level plus an electric drill, all of which were already on-site. The building under construction was a large block of flats, in addition there were a couple of houses being built at the back. It was a large and very busy site run by a company called "Robinsons". The apartment block was encased in scaffolding and, with the brickwork plus the fitting out completed one floor at a time, the project had reached the second rise.

Robinsons managed the building work from a "prefab" office on the site but, as was common practice, they hired only a few of their own workers directly and they put most of the construction work out to dozens of self-employed sub-contractors. The builders who were awarded such contracts often "subbed" the skilled work out again to specialist tradesmen such as John and Terry. For those who worked as "Subbies" this system meant that, when pay-day came around, they would receive their wages without any deductions for Income Tax or National Insurance whatsoever. This situation was so widespread throughout the construction industry that it was known colloquially as working on "The Lump". Such contrived self-employed status came with no employment rights, no trade union recognition and the limited regulations concerning health and safety were often poorly enforced. Accidents at work resulting in death or injury often ended in little or no compensation being paid to those builders forming the construction industry Lump.

When John arrived at work he found that his colleague Terry Short had already started on a new project without him. The pair of joiners had recently finished putting up door liners and hanging doors in the flats on the first floor of the property and now they were tasked with fitting the windows. There were no ladders on the scaffolding so John clambered up the metal framework to where Terry was preparing a window aperture, making it ready to receive a steel "Crittall" style frame. Whilst the scaffolding did have a waist level safety rail there was a complete absence of any kick boards to prevent objects accidentally falling from the scaffold boards to the ground five metres below. In addition, there were no rules making the wearing of hard hats compulsory, there were no trained first aiders and few if any of the site workers wore any safety clothing such as steel toe cap safety boots. The Health and Safety at Work Act did not reach the statute books until 1974.

There really wasn't any "Health and Safety" culture in those days... that was how it was then. You just went to work and got on with it. (John Kerrison)

Terry was working inside the building when John arrived. Although it was actually Terry's turn to work in the sunshine John selfishly insisted on working outside standing on the scaffolding. He told Terry that they would swop places the next day which was potentially a good tactic in view of the changeable British weather and, always the best of friends, the two joiners never argued. The window space where they were working had been prepared by the bricklayers with a load bearing reinforced concrete lintel spanning the gap at the top. This beam was designed to take the weight of the subsequent brick courses forming the upper floors of the block of flats. Fitting the Crittall windows involved drilling holes in a piece of steel attached to the lintel to which the metal frames were offered up and fixed in place with self-tapping screws. The brickwork between the bottom of the window and the floor had not yet been completed; it was intended that the area below the sill would be filled later with specially cast "fancy" bricks which would add some detail to the building's otherwise bland perfunctory facade.

Further along the building from where John was working another window had been capped with a right angled "boot" lintel. It was so called because the support beam was boot shaped in cross section like a letter "L". The boot lintel was placed with the "toe" facing outwards and then brickwork would be laid along the length of the ledge to blend in with the rest of the building and hide the greater part of the unsightly concrete beam. It was a cosmetic measure frequently employed during the early 1970s. A common cause for the failure of such boot shaped lintels was the uneven distribution of weight borne on the projecting toe which could cause the beam to tilt and become dislodged. Lintels were usually cast in situ, by pouring concrete into a wooden mould, to avoid having to raise a heavy cumbersome pre-cast reinforced concrete beam into place. Neglecting to support the mould until the concrete had become fully set could also lead to a subsequent catastrophic collapse of the lintel.

In the process of fitting one of the Crittall window frames, John knelt down to change the bit on his electric drill and that is the last thing that he remembers from that Monday morning in May 1971. It was quite some time before he was able to piece together what actually had taken place. The nearby boot lintel had shifted and fallen between the wall and the scaffolding which, with no ties securing it to the building, collapsed and threw John to the ground. It is very likely that at some point his back struck the safety rail causing him to receive a traumatic spinal injury. When he landed he also hit his head on a half brick lying on the ground which added to his injuries and, rendering him unconscious, it gave the shocking illusion that there was a whole brick embedded halfway into his skull.

In the absence of any competent trained first aider those who rushed to assist John may well have been tempted, with the best of intentions, to move him into a "more comfortable" position. This is an all too frequent occurrence at the scene of an accident and, in the case of suspected spinal injury, it can be the cause of irreversible damage to the spinal cord. Even qualified paramedics and doctors in emergency treatment hospitals have been known to make this catastrophic mistake on a patient showing symptoms of damage to the spine. However, it is not known if this happened in John's case; hitting the guard rail may have caused all the damage by itself. An ambulance arrived and took him to the Accident and Emergency Unit at Mount Vernon Hospital which, situated in Rickmansworth Road, was less than a mile away from the building site.

John was admitted to the Intensive Care Unit at Mount Vernon Hospital where he remained unconscious, probably heavily sedated with morphine, for eight days. He has a vague memory of partially waking up in agony and, after briefly glimpsing a black female nurse, lapsing back into a deep impenetrable coma following further administration of the pain controlling narcotic. The medical team at Mount Vernon Hospital delayed transferring him to a specialist spinal injuries unit until they were satisfied that they had managed to stabilise his head injury. On day nine he began to slowly regain consciousness and, very aware that he could not move or feel his legs, he became extremely concerned as to the permanency of his immobility. His parents were relieved simply by the fact that their son was still alive, it was no doubt a welcome reward for their near constant vigil by his bedside.

My dad was working away from home on a job in Derby... he came straight back to London when he heard about my accident. (John Kerrison)

It was decided that as John was no longer in a coma it was an opportune moment to transfer him to the Stoke Mandeville Hospital in Aylesbury, Buckinghamshire. He was still frustrated that he had not been given any firm details about his condition but he was also pleased to hear that he was going to Stoke Mandeville. The hospital's Spinal Injuries Unit was world famous for the near miraculous results experienced by many of its patients. Furthermore, the fame of the Buckinghamshire hospital was enhanced by one of the voluntary porters working there, a certain Mr Jimmy Saville. The BBC Radio One disc jockey and television personality had his own room at the hospital. His Herculean fund raising efforts gathered millions of pounds which eventually assisted the building of a new spinal injuries facility. This apparently altruistic work for the hospital was rewarded with an OBE followed by a knighthood bestowed by the Queen.

The realisation that I had lost the use of my legs came almost immediately... but then I told myself at the same time that things were going to be all right... I had that optimism. (John Kerrison)

John firmly believed that, in no time at all, the gifted surgeons would be able to repair his back and get his legs working again. However, the ambulance journey proved to be extremely distressing for him and he marked his arrival on the spinal injuries ward at Stoke Mandeville Hospital with a bout of uncontrollable vomiting. He drew great comfort from his devoted parents who visited him on his first night in the hospital.

Chapter Two

I used to believe in miracles as a kid... I thought that they could do miracles at Stoke Mandeville Hospital, but I don't believe it now. I hated everything about the place. (John Kerrison)

The Spinal Injuries Unit at Stoke Mandeville Hospital underwent drastic expansion in the 1940s to accommodate the large number of casualties, both soldiers and civilians, who sustained severe spinal cord injuries during the hostilities of World War II. It was run very much along strict military lines and several ground breaking rehabilitation techniques were introduced by the renowned neurologist Sir Ludwig Guttmann. The pioneering intention was to teach disabled people how to live "normal" lives, eventually gaining paid employment in order to earn their own keep. This aim to attain normality continued after the war and an impromptu sports day for spinal injury patients held within the hospital grounds in 1948, mimicking the Olympic Games held in London that year, went on to become the forerunner of the modern-day Paralympics. In that same year the hospital also became part of the newly formed National Health Service.

Spinal injuries are classified with a letter to indicate the injured area whereby "C" denotes the cervical vertebrae in the neck, "T" denotes the thoracic vertebrae in the chest, "L" denotes the lumbar vertebrae in the lower back and "S" denotes the fused sacral vertebrae at the base of the spine. In addition, the individual vertebrae in each of these spinal regions are numbered sequentially. The X-rays taken at Mount Vernon Hospital had identified the damage to John's back as being located between the eleventh and twelfth thoracic vertebrae, level with the top of his hips. This is classified as "T 11/12" and it is the most common of all such spinal injuries. In view of his lower back lesion John was placed on ward

2X at Stoke Mandeville Spinal Injuries Unit. Those diagnosed with higher lesions were generally placed on the nearby ward 1X. The male and female patients were segregated on different wards, most of those treated for spinal injury are men.

Both wards were arranged in the old fashioned "Nightingale" style with eight beds in parallel rows on each side of the unpartitioned room. This open plan arrangement facilitated patient care in that only a few medical staff were required to keep watch over everyone, the downside being that there was little privacy for the patients. There was also an annexe with four beds at the back of both wards. These rooms were used mainly by patients returning to the hospital on a short-term basis to receive further treatment for conditions such as pressure sores and urinary tract infections. Both of these ailments are common problems associated with disability following spinal injury.

At Stoke Mandeville Hospital you worked your way down the spinal injuries ward, going in at one end and coming out of the other, just like on a production line in a factory. It was run on a near military basis. Everything had a number, nothing had a name. There was a near total lack of empathy. (John Kerrison)

When John arrived at Stoke Mandeville Hospital he was still experiencing a small amount of pain in his back but it was no longer necessary for him to have morphine injections. The fracture to his skull, which had delayed his transfer to the Spinal Injuries Unit, had no long-term effects and had not even required bandaging. He spent the first three months of his stay confined to his bed in ward 2X whilst the fracture in his spine healed. The hospital bed was a strange and disconcerting contraption known as a "turning bed". It had a hinged division lengthways down the middle in order to allow either side to be raised through forty-five degrees. This novel feature enabled nursing staff to safely rotate a spinal injuries patient onto their side, then on to their front and so on. John underwent a tortuous regime of being turned every three hours, all day and all night without any respite, in order to take the pressure off his back and prevent any bed sores from forming.

In the evenings the bright fluorescent overhead lights on the ward were turned off and replaced by dimmed lighting. However, any attempts at prolonged periods of sleep were constantly interrupted because the turning process was repeated for every patient on the ward. During daylight hours a curtain was drawn around the individual patient's bed as they received nursing attention but at night such privacy, in the absence of any visitors, was deemed to be unnecessary. Everything was carried out with military precision and, despite the hospital having returned to civilian status after the war, the same ethos was applied to keeping the ward spotlessly clean. Once a week all of the beds were moved to one side and the place was scrubbed from top to bottom, one half at a time in regimental order, like a drill on a parade ground.

Patient care on the ward was executed with the same cold efficiency, usually by two nurses aided by a pair of orderlies for the heavy lifting, under the watchful eye of a severe ward sister who had previously served in the armed forces. John received physiotherapy for twenty minutes every day when a Swiss lady manipulated his legs by bending his knees and ankles. This treatment was designed to increase blood circulation and retain muscle tone as a preventative measure to combat the danger of pressure sores. The therapist was one of the few members of staff that John can remember having had even a small amount of conversation with. Nevertheless, he still felt that he was being kept completely in the dark about his situation.

John hated the hospital food served to him in his bed and, despite the "Red Cross" parcels brought in by his mother, he lost a substantial amount of body weight from his already skinny frame. He also disliked being washed in bed by the nurses, a potentially degrading process for a young man. The male patients were encouraged to shave themselves if they were able, but John's youthful beard and lack of desire to maintain his personal appearance made it a rare occurrence for him. Most spinal cord injuries result in the casualty suffering a loss of control over their bladder and bowel functions with, over a period of time, varying degrees of recovery. In John's case both these items were also dealt with in bed in a procedure which he felt robbed him of all personal dignity.

He was circumcised to facilitate the fitting of a catheter tube in order to empty his bladder and encouraged to drink plenty of fluids to reduce the risk of a urinary tract infection. Every other day he was subjected to a process termed "manual evacuation" in respect of his bowels. At Stoke Mandeville Hospital this was done in a very "by the book" approach. Nursing instruction manuals from that time read like a DIY guide describing how to carry out an oil change on a Mark II Ford Cortina. However, the clinical instructions included less regard to the patient's dignity than that suggested within the pages of any motor maintenance manual. There was nothing that John could do except lie in bed and wonder as to when such demeaning pride robbing torture was going to stop.

The spinal cord can be regarded as akin to a bundle of wires, running within a protective conduit provided by the spinal vertebrae, which transmit electronic messages to and from the brain. Catastrophic damage to this wiring in the cervical vertebrae of the neck can result in the total paralysis of the body below the break in conductivity, a condition known as quadriplegia or tetraplegia. Injury lower down the spine may lead to a paralysis of the legs which is known as paraplegia. The brain can sometimes receive "phantom" messages from receptors on areas of the body which are no longer connected by the nervous system. These erroneous signals, similar to those experienced by amputees, can be experienced as sensations of intense pain or burning heat and freezing cold. Conventional pain killers are often entirely ineffective in this situation.

Furthermore, the part of the spinal cord and the nerves separated from the brain can become hyper-excitable. This can result in various degrees of involuntary muscle movements or spasms, sometimes referred to as "Spastic Hypertonia", which are typically exhibited by uncontrollable bending or straightening of limbs despite the established paralysis. These spasms can sometimes be violent enough to throw a person from their wheelchair. John once saw a fellow paraplegic actually stand up during such a spasm. People who have incurred high lesions to the spinal cord tend to go into spasm more often than those with lower damage. In addition, conditions such as pressure sores can also increase the likelihood of a spasticity episode. In recent times the term "spastic" has fallen out of common usage due to it having been colloquially employed as a derogatory and discriminative expression in the less enlightened past.

In the States they still use the word "spastic" all the time... it doesn't seem to have the same negative connotations like it does here. (John Kerrison)

After John arrived at Stoke Mandeville Hospital no further investigative X-rays were taken of his spine and little reference was made to the X-ray plates which accompanied him from Mount Vernon. No surgery or other treatment was undertaken to restore the damage to his spinal cord except for a pillow placed under his back to provide lumbar support. These days there would probably have been some surgical attempt to correct any compression of the spinal cord by stabilising the misaligned broken vertebrae with metal pins, a process aided by the recent development of CT and MRI scans. In John's case nature was allowed to take its course and it is a matter of conjecture as to whether any surgical intervention would have produced a different result.

A friend of mine broke his neck and he was taken to the Accident and Emergency Unit. He was paralysed from the neck down and a young doctor tried to relieve the pressure on his spinal cord by manipulating his neck. Even after surgery my friend was left permanently tetraplegic... it will never be known if the medical treatment did more harm than good... but at least they tried to do something. (John Kerrison)

John spent long periods in a trance-like state, shutting out the reality of his situation, only occasionally allowing himself to ponder what the future held for him. As time went by he received little or no information concerning his condition until, around six weeks after arriving at Stoke Mandeville Hospital, he was given a particularly stark assessment by a specialist from the John Radcliffe Hospital. The brief and rather cursory appraisal, delivered with a somewhat brusque bedside manner, completely destroyed any optimism that John still held about making a full recovery.

A spinal injuries consultant came to examine me, he was called in from another hospital because I was an industrial injuries case and there were legal issues concerning the accident. I asked him,

"What's happening? Am I going to be able to walk again?" All he said to me was "That would be the thin end of the wedge". Those were the very words that he used and I took it to mean that I wasn't going to get any better. (John Kerrison)

Following this rather bizarrely worded prognosis, John descended into despair. His parents came to the hospital on a near daily basis and attempted to comfort him. In addition, both of his sisters, several relatives and friends, plus band members from The Beachcombers, were also frequent bedside visitors. Nevertheless, John felt completely alone. Linda came to see him about twice a week, she occasionally brought Simon with her but the austere environment of the spinal injuries ward was not really a suitable place to take a toddler. Nobody asked John as to whether he would ever walk again, the subject was completely avoided as if there was something rather taboo about it. He received no professional counselling whatsoever to assist him in coming to terms with his situation except for an invitation from the hospital vicar to take Holy Communion. It was an offer which John politely refused, he was never one to find solace in religious belief.

Smoking in hospital was allowed in those days and John was getting through around forty cigarettes a day in an attempt to fight the boredom and his anxiety as to what the future might hold for him. Sometimes he read a newspaper but there was little else to distract him from his negative thoughts. His parents bought him a small portable television which he watched without any real interest. Fellow smoker Jimmy Saville was a frequent sight on the ward with his well-known trademark broom handle cigar and his equally famously annoying catchphrases. The *Top of the Pops* television presenter and voluntary hospital porter was very popular amongst the patients and staff because of his incredibly successful fund raising on behalf of the Spinal Injuries Unit. His VIP status allowed him the freedom to roam the hospital at will and he would often answer requests for his autograph by immodestly writing his name as "JIMMY $AVI££E". John absolutely despised him.

Saville used to wander around getting his rocks off by pretending to help, but it was all just to feed his own ego. He saw my TV and

14

said something to me like "You're doing all right, aren't you?" As if lying on my back and being unable to walk was in any way "doing all right". That's how he was, completely false and self-centred. I told him to **** right off. (John Kerrison)

Some of John's family and friends were enthralled by seeing Jimmy Saville and they could not understand any derogatory assessments of the superstar philanthropic disc jockey. Any criticism of the highly successful fund raiser was frowned upon by the hospital staff and management who practically deified the Spinal Injuries Unit's benefactor. However, revelations after Saville's death have more than confirmed John's intuitive character judgement.

Not everyone had such a negative experience at Stoke Mandeville Hospital. John witnessed several examples of the success for which the hospital was world famous. There was an Irishman who had been injured whilst digging a deep trench on a building site. The soil had collapsed on top of him and the sheer weight left him with severe damage to his spine. After a long-term stay on ward 2X he made a near full recovery and was discharged. A short while afterwards he made a return visit to the ward and John watched him as he walked around aided only by a pair of leg callipers, the braces were probably just to give extra support in view of the muscle wastage which often results from long-term confinement to bed. John greatly resented the man's good fortune and speculated as to why he personally had not received such demonstrably successful medical treatment.

The patient in the neighbouring bed also gave John a great deal to contemplate concerning a particular aspect of his own future. Having made a full recovery from a broken neck the man was nearly ready to leave hospital and return to life in the outside world. The fortunate individual was married and his wife was a regular visitor to his bedside. On several occasions John was aware that the woman was being intimate with her husband, furtively sliding her hand under the bedclothes, and it prompted him into spending time thinking about his own destiny with regard to that subject.

I thought about it in the same way as football. Before I was paralysed from the waist down I had always liked to play football. After the accident I probably wasn't going to be able to play football

15

properly anymore but I still had a great deal of interest in the game.
(John Kerrison)

From his own personal observations, in the absence of any professional advice, John was beginning to piece together a stark vision as to what the future was likely to hold for him and he could not come to terms with it at all. He had become used to living life at full throttle in exciting times where revolution was in the air and Rock & Roll nonconformity was the new norm. John felt that his life now had no more value than a piece of dirt and perceived that those who were responsible for tending to his needs held a similar opinion. The normally gregarious extrovert Rock drummer descended into deep depression, becoming increasingly sullen and withdrawn. He considered ending it all but dismissed the idea because of the impracticality of such drastic action on an open hospital ward. There was also the possibility of recovery in an even worsened condition and, most importantly of all, the potentially devastating effect on his parents if he attempted to take his own life.

Chapter Three

People talk about all sorts of stuff as being preordained... "Was it fate that put you in a wheelchair?" they ask me. "Was it bollocks" I tell them. (John Kerrison)

It is interesting to note that these days John is unable to recall the exact date of his accident other than a reference to a nominal Monday in May 1971 despite the event having such major life-changing significance for him. To most people such anniversaries put well defined milestones into a lifetime and perhaps John's amnesia is an attempt to blot out the painful memory. Retrospective examination of the unconnected happenings on the day leading up to John's injury could easily give the appearance of orchestrated synchronicity. If any single element were to be removed from the proceedings then John would still be walking today and he would not have spent more than four decades struggling to cope with the challenges, both physical and mental, imposed by his disability. His life would have certainly been very different and, in all likelihood, it is quite possible that he would have attained the same degree of Rock & Roll renown achieved by some of his drumming contemporaries.

Adam Faith had a very bad crash driving in his Roller... he came through it all right and he said afterwards that in his mind he had blotted out the memory of what happened... it's a way of protecting yourself from how bad things were. (John Kerrison)

Thoughts concerning "What if?" and "Why me?" are part of human nature, and as John lay in his hospital bed staring at the ceiling he was tormented by such unanswerable questions. Clearly he was not to blame for the accident, the concrete lintel could have fallen at any time instead of crashing into his life. The only part that he had played in the tragic chain of events was to be in the wrong place at the wrong time. In some ways it might have been better if the injuries had been more his own fault, self-inflicted perhaps as a result of a car crash or heroically sustained fighting in a war.

My dad was an experienced joiner and he worked on several major construction projects up and down the country. He went to Maxwell Road to make his own enquiries about my accident and he was shocked to discover that the official investigators had not visited the building site until four days after the incident... most of the evidence would have been cleared away. (John Kerrison)

John turned twenty-four on 4 August 1971, it is one anniversary which he can recall with great clarity. On that occasion his wife Linda came to visit him and she brought with her a romantic birthday present. Whilst he was undergoing treatment in the Accident & Emergency Unit at Mount Vernon Hospital John's wedding ring had been removed and handed to his family. Linda had taken the gold ring to a jewellers and arranged to have the words "Happy birthday to my dearest John" engraved on the inside. It was a charming gesture which John found moving but, at the same time, he had reservations because their relationship had already begun to deteriorate before the accident. He had some suspicions that there was an ulterior motive behind the romantic gift, he detected small hints which only began to fully materialise at a later date. These days John is quite cynical and dismissive about the engraved ring. Nevertheless, he still retains the keepsake whilst adamantly denying that it is in any way a treasured memento.

After three months there was a sudden change in the hospital routine when, with little prior announcement, a wheelchair was pushed into position alongside John's bed. It was very much a defining moment, almost an induction ceremony. The wheelchair was practically antique, barely one step up from a Victorian "invalid chair". Upholstered in blue leather with substantial padding it looked like it had seen many years of service. A hard shield shaped piece of plastic was placed on John's chest and securely fastened around his back with Velcro straps. The breast plate was designed to support his trunk and, by preventing his vertebral column bending, enabled him to sit upright. Two orderlies lifted him out of bed and sat him down on the wheelchair where he initially spent about two hours.

I just sat there staring into space and thinking stuff like "This isn't me" and "It shouldn't be happening to me" plus a lot of other self-destroying thoughts. It was heavy, heavy... a very low point in my life. (John Kerrison)

John wore the uncomfortable spinal brace for about two to three weeks and throughout that period being lifted into the wheelchair became a daily event. He was never left to sit in the chair for more than a few hours a day due to the risk of forming pressure sores, and he was unable to move away from his bedside as the wheelchair was not the type which could be propelled by the occupant. When his parents saw him sitting upright they were very pleased, probably because it indicated to them that their son was making progress. However, John did not regard it as any real improvement in his situation and he hated his visitors seeing him in a wheelchair. He felt embarrassed by the obvious demonstration of his disablement.

The hospital then issued John with his own wheelchair. It was a model made by a company called "Everest and Jennings", and they dominated the wheelchair market in the fifties and sixties with their lightweight foldaway designs. Castor wheels at the front of the wheelchair enhanced its manoeuvrability and handrail rims on the large rear wheels enabled him to move around and explore his surroundings. John hated the hospital food which he had been served with when confined to his bed and therefore being able to visit the canteen was something of a blessing. He became a regular customer and often purchased cups of tea, cheese rolls and Mars bars which went some way to restoring his lost bodyweight. On one occasion John's uncle took him for a drive with the wheelchair folded away in the boot of his Ford Anglia. It was a welcome break from the boredom of being stuck in the suspended animation of life in hospital.

John's newly found mobility led to him encountering another resident in the Spinal Injuries Unit. The young Scotsman had been injured whilst celebrating his twenty-first birthday. Troublemakers had gatecrashed his party and he fell off a roof whilst attempting to escape when a fight started. As a result of the fall he sustained a broken neck which, diagnosed as a high cervical vertebrae "C" lesion, rendered him completely tetraplegic with absolutely no hope of any recovery. Plans were underway to transfer him to a residential spinal unit in Musselburgh, a small Scottish coastal town near Edinburgh, where he would probably spend the rest of his days. He had no family to go to and, even if he did have relatives to care for him, any attempt at home nursing would have proven very difficult in view of the demanding needs imposed by his near helpless condition.

The young man was in a deep suicidal depression and John, together with some of the other mobile patients, assisted him into maintaining a drunken stupor by supplying him with copious amounts of booze. They also fitted him with plenty of "leg bags" to accommodate the additional urine that he produced as a result of his drinking binges. John's own disability was nowhere near as severe and, in contrast to the tetraplegic Scotsman, he also had an extensive network of supportive relatives and friends. However, John drew no consolation from seeing someone worse off than himself and, despite having a great deal of empathy for the unfortunate young man, he did not identify himself as being a "fellow" member of the disabled. Furthermore, he did not socialise much with the other spinal injuries patients, theirs was a fraternity which he had not joined by choice.

John had grown up in a society which, at that time, possessed few of the politically correct values which are demanded by present day attitudes and enforced by legal statutes. When he was at school he and his friends frequently employed the discriminatory expressions which were in common usage. This included words such as "spaz", "spacker", "crip" and also the rhyming slang "raspberry ripple" for cripple. In addition, there was also a widespread belief that anyone with a physical disability also suffered from impaired mental ability. John recalls that the children travelling by mini bus to the "Special School" were referred to as "window lickers". Prejudice usually results from both ignorance and fear of the unknown; in this case it can be traced back to the Victorian practice of isolating the disabled in institutions adhering to a policy of "out of sight and out of mind". The ambition at Stoke Mandeville Hospital was completely the opposite, their aim was for integration and a semblance of "normality" for their patients.

I am not "a disabled person", I am "a person with a disability". I am no more "confined to a wheelchair" than anyone is confined to their shoes. However, I don't really care what anyone calls me. I hate all of the "Politically Correct" stuff because it's often just lip service... What really matters to me is feeling included and to be treated with respect. (John Kerrison)

John was soon visiting the Physiotherapy Department every day, wheeling himself there to work out on the weights and muscle building pulley machines plus some of the other exercise equipment. The manipulation of his legs, bending and stretching, also continued as part of his therapy. Swimming was also thought to be of great benefit and John received treatment in the hydrotherapy pool where the heated water, warmed to body temperature, aided exercise by increasing blood circulation. There was a transfer chair to lift the patient into and out of the pool which in reality was more like a big tiled bath. John disliked the hydrotherapy sessions because of the difficulty that he experienced in getting changed and sorting out his leg bag. He recalls being treated with a lack of sensitivity, as if he was a "thing" rather than a vulnerable and frightened person.

As kids we used to go down to the swimming pool in Heston and mess about... I could swim, but not that well... I didn't enjoy the swimming therapy at Stoke Mandeville... there was no freedom to actually swim and also no empathy from the therapists. Anyway, it's all a waste of time if you can't mess about and jump in. (John Kerrison)

There was a high degree of emphasis placed on exercise and sporting activity as part of the rehabilitation process at Stoke Mandeville Hospital. John was encouraged to play table tennis and to indulge in pursuits such as archery in the hospital's extensive grounds. Most afternoons there were also occupational therapy sessions which were designed to assist in returning the patients to paid employment. This took the form of activities including sewing, painting and sawing bits of wood. Little attempt was made to customise the training for a patients particular needs. John felt that the tasks that he was set were particularly trivial, patronising and insulting for a skilled carpenter. He didn't want to have occupational training, table tennis and archery. What John wanted to do was to play football and work as a joiner, but most of all he wanted to play the drums in a Rock & Roll band.

It was rubbish, everything was rubbish. I could not get my head around any of it. All it did was emphasise to me that I had lost both my trades, as drummer and also as a joiner... I felt like a piece of worthless rubbish. (John Kerrison)

The purpose of the intensive muscle building exercises became apparent when John was measured for a pair of leg callipers. Improving his upper body strength, which had diminished after three months confined to a bed, was a precursor to his being trained to walk using orthotic supports. This was very much in line with the Stoke Mandeville obsessive ethos of restoring "normality". The tailor made leg callipers consisted of steel rods which, attached with leather straps, rigidly braced Johns legs from his feet to his groin. Leather bindings encased each of his knees where a hinge in the assembly allowed the joint to be bent, when the wearer was in a sitting position, or to be locked to keep the leg straight when standing up. Johns shoes were fitted with a special heel which had a spigot in which to fix the steel rods and his upper body weight was supported on top of a hard leather pad under his crutch.

At that time leg callipers were often associated with Polio. Following a major outbreak of the crippling viral disease in the 1950s many children had been left with weak and deformed legs. Subsequently a mass vaccination programmes practically eradicated the epidemic but there was something of a stigma attached to the condition. John recalls that as a child he was scared of the life sized figurine of a boy in leg callipers which, standing outside a local shop, had a coin slot in the head to accept charitable donations on behalf of the Spastic Society. There was also a pupil at John's school who wore leg callipers as a result of the birth defect Spina Bifida. John and his schoolmates got on well enough with him but the boy was somewhat isolated by his inability to play football and their other robust games. It was only through the insistence of the physiotherapists at Stoke Mandeville that John reluctantly agreed to try wearing the cumbersome heavy leg braces.

The 1954 biographical movie *"Reach for the Sky"* tells the story of Douglas Bader who lost both his legs after crashing his aircraft and, after learning to walk again using prosthetic legs, went on to become a World War II "Ace" fighter pilot. In one scene the heroic RAF Officer, portrayed with a great deal of thespian ham by actor Kenneth More, stoically struggles to take his first tentative steps using his artificial limbs. The situation was much more challenging for John in that Bader was an amputee rather than a paraplegic and could therefore raise his prosthetic limbs using the remaining stumps of his legs. John could only employ the muscles in his upper body when he was attempting to walk in leg callipers, raising his foot off the floor by hoisting his hip. He practised the technique whilst grasping hold of the parallel bars in the physiotherapy unit until he graduated to using crutches.

It is very difficult to walk or even to remain standing without the use of leg muscles which, in normal circumstances, make the constant subtle compensatory adjustments required to maintain balance. There are two main methods of walking in leg callipers which attempt to overcome this problem. "Swing through" involves placing both crutches on the floor in front of the feet and then, as the name suggests, swinging the legs forward together. The other system is called "four point" whereby the right crutch is placed forward followed by the left leg and then the process is repeated with the left crutch and then the right leg. In John's case both types of walking placed a huge strain on his midriff, often sending his stomach into an uncontrollable spasm which caused him to vomit. The involuntary contraction of his abdominal muscles also pulled him forward and made him overbalance.

On one occasion when John was wearing the leg callipers the exertion from using his shoulder muscles to lift the heavy metal work put considerable pressure on his bowels. With no feeling in his legs the embarrassing result only became apparent to him when he glanced down at his feet. It was another low moment for the young man and, despite the Stoke Mandeville ethos to become "normal", he

23

eventually decided to give up trying to master walking in the callipers. The expensive orthotics were donated to a charity in Africa where they may well have been of more use to someone who, following less damaging spinal injury, had retained at least some small amount of muscle control to operate their hips or knees.

Chapter Four

Everything about Stoke Mandeville Hospital was so negative for me. I felt like I had a destroyed life and there was no psychological content to help me to adjust mentally... The attitude was just "get on with it and do it"... Fortunately it isn't like that anymore. (John Kerrison)

After John had spent around four months at Stoke Mandeville Hospital he was considered to be well enough to start going home at weekends. He was picked up from the hospital by his friend Peter Veryard and, assisted by his brother-in-law Chris, driven to his council maisonette in Cranford Drive Hayes. The flat was on the second floor and so John had to endure the embarrassment of being carried bodily up the stairs by his two friends. It soon became very apparent that, as a consequence of his disability, it was no longer a suitable place for him to live. In the absence of any modifications to essential items such as the toilet and washing facilities John was left to try and manage as best as he could.

Linda hated the sight of her husband's wheelchair just as much as he did and, when John was staying at home, it was hidden away in a cupboard by mutual agreement. John sat on the sofa all day and he slept on it at night, he was bored out of his mind and the weekends became a torture for him. He is very critical of the lack of ability and enthusiasm that his wife showed as a carer but, in fairness to Linda, it should be noted that she also had a demanding toddler to look after. They put in an application to the Housing Department at Hillingdon Council for rehousing in more suitable accommodation, something that would better suit the needs of a wheelchair user, but weeks later John had still not received a response. The weekend home visits put a considerable amount of pressure on a relationship which was apparently already under a great deal of strain prior to the accident.

After one really bad weekend at home I went back to the hospital feeling very depressed. Instead of going to a physiotherapy session I went off on my own and chain-smoked a load of cigarettes. The next day the physiotherapist had a right go at me for not turning up... I tried to explain that I couldn't cope with it all, my marital situation and everything else, but it was no good... At Stoke Mandeville they weren't interested in my mental condition... the attitude was "just get on with it". (John Kerrison)

Near the end of John's stay at Stoke Mandeville Hospital he went home for one more weekend before he was due to be discharged. He was shocked when he found out that although Hillingdon Council had offered to move the family, to a house which had been converted to cater for his disability, Linda had kept the matter quiet and she had also failed to accept the offer. In the argument that followed some sharp words were exchanged culminating with Linda stating that she was not happy with the situation and that she wanted a separation. John was distraught and he threw himself off the sofa and onto the floor. He bumped along on his backside through the front door and out onto the balcony with the intention of falling to his death. Fortunately he was unable to complete his desperate attempt at suicide.

When I returned to Stoke Mandeville Hospital they found that I had developed two really bad pressure sores on my backside from where I bashed myself on the floor. I had to stay for a couple of weeks longer than was intended, lying in bed, in order to receive treatment. (John Kerrison)

Around seven months after the accident, on Christmas Eve 1971, John was finally discharged from Stoke Mandeville. It was decided that he should go back to live with his parents, in the same house where he was born and raised, until his marital difficulties were hopefully resolved. A neighbour called Sid Foreman picked John up from the hospital and drove him home with his wheelchair folded up in the boot, on the way home they stopped at a pub. Sid was a friend of the family and had been the manager of a band which John had played in when he was still at school. Reminiscing about the old days over a drink temporarily gave the situation a sense of normality but they sat together in the car rather than in the pub. John didn't want to go through the hassle of getting into his wheelchair and he was also embarrassed to be seen in public.

When John arrived at his parent's council house he had to be lifted indoors because of the steps leading up to the front door prevented him entering on his wheelchair, it was only the beginning of the many challenges which he was about to face. He sat on the three seater settee in the front room and, copying the arrangement in his own flat, he slept on it in the evenings. Christmas was always a big event in the Kerrison household and it was very likely that the usual festive decorations were in place, plus there would have been plenty of relatives and family friends visiting the house. John didn't notice or join in with any of the traditional merriment, he felt that he had very little to celebrate. The familiar surroundings did nothing to alleviate his deep depression.

Norman Mitchener was very upset when he heard about John's accident and he tried to help him as much as possible. The Beachcombers' guitarist repeatedly went to see Linda, taking her presents of flowers and chocolates, in an attempt to patch things up but it was to no avail. There were no reconciliation meetings or any professional counselling and it appeared that the marriage was over. Furthermore, Linda was refusing all offers from John's family to act as baby sitters when she went out for the evening. This raised suspicions that she was attempting to hide the fact that she was seeing another man. John still kept in contact with his adopted son Simon, his father or his older sister would regularly collect the boy and take him back to the house. The three year old toddler was probably oblivious to the drama unfolding around him.

Once the rumours started to surface that his wife was having an affair John took it quite badly. When Linda had given him the engraved wedding ring as a birthday present he had questioned the motive behind the gift but the confirmation that something was wrong still came as a shock. He felt that he had made a commitment to their relationship which he would have honoured come what may and he had expected the same from his wife. In his mind he was certain that, had their roles been reversed, he would have found a way to cope with the situation. The next time that he saw Linda was many years later when, at Simon's wedding reception, she unexpectedly walked up and kissed him.

If the roles had been reversed then I would have looked after her... because it was what I took on, it was the commitment that I made... It was not a joint decision to split up and that was wrong... I don't go back on my word and I don't lie. (John Kerrison)

A month or so after moving into his parents' house John began going to Hillingdon Hospital, an ambulance took him for regular physiotherapy and occupational therapy sessions. He still held a small amount of optimism that he might undergo a full or partial recovery. John's transfer from Stoke Mandeville was arranged following his very vocal protests that he did not wish to ever return there. However, he still had to go back to Stoke Mandeville every six months for an IVP "intravenous pyelogram", a radiological procedure employed to detect irregularities and problems in the kidneys, bladder and ureters. Such monitoring programmes are routinely carried out following permanent spinal cord damage. The IVP test involves injecting an opaque dye into the blood stream and a sequence of X-rays follows the progress of the pigment as it is excreted through the urinary system. These days the system has been largely replaced by ultra sound equipment. John hated retuning to Stoke Mandeville, he was particularly concerned that they might discover something else wrong with him which would lead to his long-term readmission.

At Stoke Mandeville the level of psychological care was very poor. It was all about "he is a C6" and "he is a T4" according to your condition and not who you were... they were very cold and impersonal. None of them were disabled and they had no idea what I was going through mentally or physically. (John Kerrison)

When it became apparent that John would probably be living at his parents' house on a permanent basis he moved from the front room to the dining room. His old bed was brought down from the bedroom where he used to sleep before he left home to get married; it was almost certainly a lot more comfortable than sleeping on the sofa. With no accessible toilet facilities John had to rely on a commode which, when in disguise from its primary function, doubled up as a chair; he rarely spent any time sitting in his wheelchair. For John's mother it was almost like having a child to nurse again, a situation which she stoically managed whilst also holding down a job at the same time.

A short while after the accident John began to receive Industrial Injuries Disablement Benefit which, although totalling less than the high earnings that he commanded as a skilled joiner, still gave him financial independence. The benefit was paid to John by the Department of Health and Social Security, after an assessment by a Consultant in the Spinal Injuries Unit at Stoke Mandeville Hospital found that he was no longer able to work as a result of the injuries that he had sustained. There was a certain amount of stigma attached to living on "state handouts" and John questioned as to why he was being paid so much money for doing nothing. His mother told him that he was entitled to the disability pension and, because he had always paid his self-employed National Insurance stamp, it was his as a right.

When I had the accident I didn't have all my National Insurance stamps paid up to date. I was four weeks behind and my mother told Linda to get the stamps paid quick just in case it made a difference. I had no life insurance... I should have, but the money did not always stretch that far... The man from the Prudential was always visiting my mum's house. (John Kerrison)

The Volga car seemed somewhat redundant and it was sold to a friend's uncle who lived in Catford. However, John's drum kit presented a much greater dilemma and selling it must have been an extremely hard decision for him to make, coming to terms emotionally with the depressing fact that he would never play the drums again. It is quite possible to play the snare drum, tom toms and cymbals in a drum kit using only the hands. However, John was a Rock & Roll drummer and that genre of percussion is defined by the accentuated back beat provided by the bass drum. Normally a Rock drummer would use their right foot on a pedal to play the bass drum with their left foot operating the top hat cymbals. John's paralysis prevented him from using foot pedals and, at that time, he believed that there was no practical way of circumventing the problem. Eventually he sold all of his drum kit except for the Ludwig snare drum which he kept and still owns today, he used the money to buy a decent quality record deck and amplifier plus a stereo speaker system.

John buried himself away in the back room and, despite the best efforts of his family and friends, he lived like a hermit. He was very fortunate to have so much support but at the time he did not fully appreciate it. Most days he would stay in bed until around midday when his mother returned home from work. She would help him get up and perform his ablutions, keeping him clean with a blanket bath. Then he would just mess around reading magazines and playing records before going back to bed at about 7.00 pm. In the evenings he preferred to be on his own while his parents would be watching television in the front room. Sitting down for long periods of time exacerbated the bed sores on John's buttocks and he began to spend more and more time in bed.

I was lonely at home, even with my parents and family around me, because I wasn't the John that I used to be. I wasn't the walking talking loud idiot John Kerrison that I should have been. I was just this disabled guy. (John Kerrison)

John's pressure sores, known as "decubitus ulcers", refused to heal and they were giving serious cause for concern. Sitting in the same spot for too long can cut off the blood circulation with damaging consequences for the affected tissue which in effect starts to die. Normally when this occurs the resulting pain encourages a change in position. However, in the case of severe spinal injury there is no sensation felt and the damage increases, eventually forming a sore. Furthermore, the lack of muscle tone and the weight loss following paralysis gives less protective padding to the affected area. Poor circulation from lack of movement also slows the healing process and there is a real danger of septicaemia, a bacterial blood poisoning which can lead to organ failure with potentially fatal consequences. A district nurse visited John at home every few weeks to treat and monitor his sores. He disliked her intensely, she appeared to have little understanding of the problems that he faced and a complete lack of empathy towards his disability.

At the same time as John's physical health deteriorated so did his mental health. His feelings of low self worth increased to the point where he again began to consider harming himself, he was not happy with what he had become and he wanted an exit route. It was only a decade since the 1961 Suicide Act had been passed and, despite the change in law which ended the prosecution of those who survived an attempt to kill themselves, a great deal of shame and disgrace still surrounded the subject. Such consequences and the affect on his family persuaded John against taking such drastic action but he began to misdirect his anger towards his mother and, to a lesser extent, towards his father.

The doctor was called and he paid one of his rare home visits to examine John. He performed a rather disinterested and perfunctory diagnosis of John's mental illness before prescribing antidepressant tablets. The pharmaceutical product was almost certainly Valium, the use and abuse of the diazepam tranquilliser was so widespread in the 1970s that it became a cultural icon. Handed out to countless depressed housewives the drug inspired the Rolling Stone's hit single "Mother's Little Helper".

The pills took a long time to work and they used to put me in a trance like a zombie… I was always falling asleep… It was a very meagre existence. (John Kerrison)

After a month or so he stopped taking the soporific medication and substituted the doctor's prescription with a much less legal alternative. One of John's former associates regularly supplied him with a large lump of cannabis resin free of charge. John smoked the narcotic straight, without the addition of tobacco, in a large church warden style pipe. Getting stoned in the evening while listening to records on his stereo system became a regular part of his routine. If his parents were aware that he was smoking cannabis they never mentioned it. In any event the pungent odour was probably a dead giveaway.

Late at night John would plug in his headphones so that his stereo system would not disturb his mother who had to be up early in the morning to go to work. Prior to his accident he rarely had the time to

31

listen to much music but now he was building quite an impressive collection of LP records. John recalls listening to albums from various bands including "Focus", "Steely Dan", "The Eagles", "Chicago", "Blood Sweat and Tears", "The Allman Brothers", "Jefferson Airplane", and so on. It was a rather eclectic mix of Heavy Rock, Country Rock and Pop musical genres. One of the bands that John particularly admired was "Deep Purple", their legendary album "Machine Head" was released in 1972. John also admired the work of Deep Purple drummer Ian Paice, especially for his drumming on the earlier single "Black Knight". However, he found it difficult to listen to the band's music because it invoked too many connections to his past life, too many memories and too many painful thoughts of what could have been.

Machine Head had been released less than a year after John had received his catastrophic spinal injury and he was very envious of Deep Purple's success. Before the accident he had played alongside the band's vocalist Ian Gillan and the bass guitarist Roger Glover in a group called "Episode Six". Both of them and several other of John's former associates were now internationally famous Rockstars. Theirs was an achievement and lifestyle that he had obsessively desired since he was twelve years old. Touring the world, having money, fast cars, a nice house and doing things the way that he wanted to had always been his ultimate goal. The accident had robbed him of all chances of achieving his ambition, it was like suffering a bereavement.

I met drummer Ian Paice a few years ago after a Deep Purple concert. I told him that he should be very proud of the iconic drum fill that he did on their hit single "Black Knight" and I asked him how he did it. He said that he was drunk at the time and that somehow it just happened. (John Kerrison)

In 1972 Nilsson's "Without You", a cover of a track by the British band "Badfinger", made its way to the top of the UK pop charts. The morbidly emotional lyrics resonated with John's own feelings concerning everything that he had lost. He played the song over and over again, wallowing in his own self pity.

Part II - Before the Accident

Chapter Five

My mum always told me "Never be a sheep John, don't baa baa with everyone else"... So I didn't. (John Kerrison)

John Kerrison was born on Monday 4 August 1947 upstairs in the front bedroom at number 50 Botwell Common Road, Hayes, Middlesex. Although he has always answered to the name "John" his parents, Ernest and Clare, actually named their son "Ernest John Henry Kerrison" and that is how he was baptised at St Mary's Church in Hayes. Ernest is also the forename that appears on his birth certificate, on his passport and on most of his other official documents. Having the same first name as his father soon started to cause confusion in the Kerrison household. When Mrs Kerrison became tired of referring to her son as "Little Ern" and his father as "Big Ern" she began calling him "John". The sobriquet stuck and "John" Kerrison is the name that he has been known by ever since, both privately and professionally. He speaks with great warmth in his voice when talking about his parents and his two siblings, an older sister called Annette Rosemary and a younger sister called Barbara Irene; all the Kerrison children were born within three years of one another. Furthermore, when discussing his childhood, John frequently mentions that he was "spoilt rotten".

The family home, a three bedroom semi-detached council house, was newly built in 1947 and completed just in time for the Kerrisons to take up residence before John's birth. This was a prime example of the extraordinary post World War II boom, in both the birth rate and the construction of social housing, which followed the return of the men who had previously been fighting on the front line overseas. John's father had himself been called up and served with the British Army (The Royal Dragoons) attempting to keep the peace in trouble torn Palestine prior to the formation of the state of Israel. It could be said that Mr Ernest Kerrison was actually born into the military because his mother gave birth to him in an Army drill hall in Heckmondwike, Yorkshire. Furthermore, his father was a Regimental Sergeant Major and both of his brothers joined different regiments in the British Army. After being given a medical discharge from the Armed Forces, on account of a childhood chest condition, John's father returned to his trade working as a joiner. Despite his pulmonary problems he still managed to smoke sixty cigarettes a day.

My great uncle Major A. V. Kerrison, my dad's uncle, was a mathematician... during the Second World War, whilst serving in the British Army, he invented the "Kerrison Predictor". It was an anti aircraft gun sight which helped shoot down low flying enemy planes. (John Kerrison)

John's mother originally hailed from Hornchurch, Essex and had entered "Upstairs, Downstairs" style domestic service as a young girl before the war. She was introduced to her future husband, despite their geographical separation, when her mother's brother married Ernest's second eldest sister. They began married life living in Ernest's eldest sister's house, where their first child Annette was born, before being assigned their own home by Hayes Council. As a couple Mr and Mrs Kerrison were just as opposite to one another in character as the conflicting polarity of their north and south origins, he was quiet and reserved whilst she was very outspoken. Both parents had one trait in common, they consistently supported all three of their children in everything that they wanted to achieve. The Kerrisons were always a very close-knit family.

It is very obvious that John inherited his mother's forthright manner whereas both his sisters apparently tended to mirror their father's contrasting placid nature. Eldest sister Annette was the studious, serious type and later had a high flying career which included working for the Exxon Oil Company in Libya. Younger sister Barbara showed great talent early on as a sculptor and painter. She married at seventeen and, in a business partnership with her husband, she eventually became a successful antiques dealer. Both of John's parents passed away in the 1980s. His mother left behind a recording in which she detailed her early life but John has never heard it played. He has been denied access to the tape by his eldest sister who, still ever protective towards her younger brother, maintains that it would make him feel far too sad.

After leaving the Army John's father worked for the Wimpey Construction Company who were laying concrete for a new runway at Heathrow Airport. Another job as a joiner involved a ten mile bike ride to Paddington. The family dog was a small black mongrel called "Tiny" who was not allowed in the house and slept in the garden shed. He would faithfully accompany his master to work, running alongside him as he cycled there and back home again. Later, in search of higher wages, Mr Kerrison took a job with Taylor Woodrow working on the nuclear power stations being built around the country which included Calder Hall in Cumbria, Hinkley Point in Somerset and Sizewell in Suffolk. He worked away from home for periods of up to six weeks which John remembers as being an insufferably long time when he was a small boy waiting for his father's return.

When John went on a school trip to see the famous caverns at Cheddar Gorge in Somerset he got an extra surprise when his father, who was working at Hinkley Point Power Station, arranged to meet him. The teachers gave special permission for him to stay with his father who was living at lodgings nearby in Bridgewater. The summer holidays sometimes provided another chance for the family to be reunited. Some years they would all go to the West Country in dad's green Austin A30 and stay in bed and breakfast guest houses. The car was only a small two door saloon and the Kerrison children would have to clamber over the front seats to sit together in the back. John recalls wearing knitted swimming trunks on the beach, they had an unfortunate tendency to fall down when they got soaked in the sea.

It was always a full house come Christmas time at the Kerrisons, all of John's aunts and uncles plus his cousins and his grandmother would be there. The front room normally remained unused for most of the year, to keep it in pristine condition, but on special occasions it was thrown open to receive visitors and to host parties. In the days before most people had a television they used to entertain themselves by playing all the old fashioned parlour games. John recalls a family favourite called "the tea-pot game", a pastime with unfathomable idiosyncratic rules which are long forgotten. On Christmas Day everybody gathered around the radio to hear King George VI address the nation in a tradition which, after his death in 1952, was continued by his daughter Queen Elizabeth II.

When the houses were built in Botwell Common Road the undeveloped fields on the other side of the street, known as Purser's Farm, were used to grow diverse crops including cabbages and wheat. The arable land stretched down to border the Grand Union Canal which carried cargo loaded narrow boats right up into the sixties, some of which were still horse drawn. Situated at the end of the residential road was "Lake Farm Park" which had previously constituted the lavish gardens of a stately mansion belonging to a family of Hayes gentry whose surname was "Shackles". The impressive house has long gone and the estate has become classified as a country park. These open spaces provided an ideal playground for John and his group of five friends comprising "best mate" Myles Lee, two brothers called Derek and Keith Radburn plus Rodney "Razor" Keen.

I tried fishing in the Grand Union Canal once with my mates but I got bored after a quarter of an hour and left, I've never had much patience. The Pack Hills, as we called it, was where they put all of the spoil when they dug out the canal and we used to play there a lot. (John Kerrison)

The area where John lived was predominantly working class in those days, there were few cars and only a small amount of passing traffic to interrupt the boys when they were playing football in the street. A local character called Chikka Murphy drove an American car and dressed as a Teddy Boy. It was rumoured that he was a gangster but John never found out if that was true; nevertheless he and his young friends always stopped playing and got out of the way quickly if they saw a big "Yank" motorcar coming down the road. One of John's neighbours, a Mr Foreman, had a motorcycle and sidecar combination which was more often than not off the road and, reduced to its constituent components, undergoing repair following numerous breakdowns. John and his friends built their own go-kart from a wooden soapbox and some old pram wheels; the ramshackle contraption kept falling apart and required constant maintenance.

However, by far the most common mode of transport was the bicycle. This was demonstrated every morning by the hoards of workers cycling to work at the nearby Thorn EMI factory where they used to manufacture radiograms and the "His Master's Voice" (HMV) gramophone records. All the men carried their lunch in old khaki rucksacks which presumably had originally been issued to them when they had served in the Armed Forces. Furthermore, on match days the car park at Hayes football club was full of bikes. John's mother also rode her bicycle to get to the "Wall's" sausage factory and meat processing plant in Hayes where she was employed as a pastry cook in the workers' canteen.

Mrs Kerrison would set off to work early in the morning, whilst John and his sisters were still fast asleep in their beds. Shirley Readon, their next door neighbours' teenage daughter, was tasked with waking the children and preparing breakfast before sending them off to school. John would meet up with Myles and they would kick a tennis ball, passing it back and forth between them, all the way to the strangely named "Dr Triplett's Primary School". After lessons John would again repeat his football practice on the way home where his mother, having completed her shift at the Wall's workers' canteen, would be waiting for him. Annette and Barbara both ate school dinners but the food was not to John's taste, he describes the meals as being "terrible". Mrs Kerrison, ever willing to spoil her son, responded by arranging for him to have his lunch at her friend's house; a neighbour called Mrs Currie. That there was a great sense of community in the street was also demonstrable by the fact that practically no one locked their front door when they went out.

Mrs Currie and her Scots husband "Jock" had an exceptionally large brood comprising thirteen children. John remembers them as being very nice people and also that they "didn't have two halfpennies to rub together". However, at that time he witnessed little of the extreme poverty and poor health experienced by preceding generations. This was mainly thanks to the newly introduced Welfare State which included a National Health Service and, to combat the leg deforming condition called Rickets, there was also free school milk. Subsequent vaccination programmes did a great deal to combat TB and virtually eradicated the crippling viral disease Poliomyelitis.

Victorian attitudes of embarrassment and fear towards disability were still widely prevalent, leading to an institutionalising policy of "out of sight and out of mind". John admits that he felt uncomfortable whenever he saw someone who was disabled, he would even cross the road to avoid walking past the frightening mannequin of a small boy in leg callipers, designed to collect charitable donations, which stood outside a local shop. The banter in the school playground frequently involved the use of words like "crip" and "spaz" as derogatory terms to describe poor physical or mental ability.

At lunchtime the radio in the Currie household was usually tuned to the BBC "Light Programme" and John remembers one song in particular.

I was probably around about eight years old, that sort of age, when I heard Tony Bennett singing "Stranger in Paradise" and then bang... something must have clicked inside of me because of the melody... it must have been deeply subliminal in some way because it just stayed there. (John Kerrison)

Lessons at primary school included musical activities but, at that time, John showed no more than the usual wide eyed interest that all small boys exhibit when given a drum to play. He also paid scant attention towards the upright piano at home except when his mother played it, especially when she vamped up the tunes that he liked to hear. Both of his sisters had piano lessons for a short while but they stopped attending the classes, apparently because of the inappropriate "hands on" teaching style employed by their tutor. John cannot remember why the piano was taken away, nor was he unduly upset when it went, he was far more interested in football; a passion not shared by his father. As a rabid supporter of the Arsenal FC, and local team Hayes, John's boyhood hero was the Gunners and Welsh

International goalkeeper Jack Kelsey. John and his friends always had a ball to play with, he usually played in goal but he describes his own performance as "poor". He recalls that on one occasion when he was in goal for Dr Triplett's they lost eleven nil to a team from Yeading Juniors. A boy called Alan Barratt scored a hat trick, he later became the lead singer for the British band called "Jo Jo Gunne".

Another very popular hobby at that time was train-spotting. John and his group of five friends would go to Liverpool Street Station, Euston or King's Cross with a packed lunch. They spent all day diligently recording the names and train numbers of the Hall Class and the Castle Class steam locomotives in their note books. Holiday trips to the West Country enabled John to add GWR Manor Class engines to his tally. On Saturdays John and his chums would all go to the pictures at the Ambassador Cinema in Hayes town. Cowboy films such as the "Lone Ranger" plus others such as "Zorro" and "Casey Jones" were their favourites. The boys all emulated their big screen heroes and John's most treasured toy was a pirate style double barrelled flintlock pistol, despite one of the hammers having been broken. At the age of nine he started building a Hornby train set. The track was laid out on a large board which had to be set up every time it was played with and then put away afterwards, it was a somewhat inconvenient arrangement.

Near to where John lived there was a large property called Wistowe House where one of his school friends called John Harris lived. His mother ran the place as a lodging house for working men and she always appeared to be busy cooking meals for them or cleaning the rooms. Her husband worked as an accountant and ran his business from an office around the back of the house where, acting like a magnet on John and his mates, there was also a model railway laid out in the garden. In the main house there was a small hall where Mr Fripp, a relative of the Harris family, gave dancing lessons. There were murals of desert island palm trees on the walls and the dance hall became a popular venue for bands in the 1960s. At the front of the building there was a small grocery store. Ian Mould was another local boy, his father ran the Royal Oak pub which was situated just fifty yards from Wistowe House. Next to the pub in

Church Road was the Hayes FC football ground where the social club became the "Blue Moon" at weekends.

The purchase of sweets was officially rationed by the government during the war, in order to combat shortages, and the draconian measure continued until 1953. One day after school John and his best friend Myles found half a crown (12.5 new pence) on the ground in Hayes Park after the carnival. He remembers that they went straight to a shop where they spent their windfall on sweets and then scoffed the lot. On another occasion John and another friend from primary school called Geoffrey Littlefield each stole a 5d (2 new pence) Mars bar from the Post Office shop in Church Walk Hayes. They were caught and when a horrified Mrs Kerrison was informed about her son's larceny she decided that the crime merited severe punishment. Every week for five weeks John and Geoffrey had to each repay one penny to the shopkeeper and receive a whack on the hand as a punishment for the crime; being spoilt as a child did not include parental tolerance of serious misbehaviour.

Dr Triplett's Primary was a Church of England "State" school which meant that there were compulsory classes in Religious Education plus once a week all of the children attended a service at the nearby St Mary's Church. John attempted to join the church choir but was rejected because he apparently sang "like a trumpet gone wrong". He subsequently took confirmation classes and became an altar boy where he misused his position to mischievously steal the communion wine. By the time he went to senior school he had decided that orthodox religious belief held little or no relevance for him. However, an incident whilst on holiday at the seaside with his mother and grandmother led to a profound spiritual conversion. The jukebox in an amusement arcade on the pier was playing "Runaway" by Del Shannon and John listened to it over and over again as if he was entranced, he had discovered Rock & Roll. His worship of the rhythmic music with its accentuated back beat quickly turned into an obsessive commitment that would last a lifetime. Furthermore, no matter what befell him in the years that followed, John Kerrison always kept the faith.

Chapter Six

*I didn't learn any music at secondary school at all. They had
music lessons, a choir and an orchestra run by a teacher called Mr
Trant... but it was all "Tchaikovsky with violins" and the rest of that
old rubbish. It just wasn't for me because by that time that I had
found Rock & Roll.* (John Kerrison)

Mellow Lane Comprehensive School in Hayes End was apparently
one of the first of its kind to be trialled in the radical post war
reformation of the state educational system. John's somewhat
mediocre performance at primary school improved dramatically
when he moved to the new style secondary school. Whilst he found
some of the more academic subjects quite challenging he excelled in
the technical subjects, especially those that involved using his hands,
such as metalwork and woodwork. John particularly enjoyed Games
and PE lessons and he later went on to gain a place in the school
football team as a goalkeeper.

Despite being at the forefront of progressive education Mellow
Lane Comprehensive School still retained corporal punishment as a
deterrent against bad behaviour. Although John claims to have been a
reasonably well behaved pupil he admits to having been beaten with
a slipper on numerous occasions for infringements including not
having clean football boots, forgetting to bring his games kit,
messing about in the changing rooms and trying to take a peek when
the girls were showering. The cane was employed for those caught
smoking or for fighting and other more serious offences. John recalls
a disciplinarian art teacher at the school called Mr Turner; he dressed
in a style that was fashionable at that time, including a drape jacket
and "drain pipe" trousers, which earned him the nick name "Teddy-
boy Turner".

Fellow pupils who attended Mellow Lane Comprehensive include Steve Priest (who went on to achieve fame as the bass guitarist in the band "Sweet"), John Sissons (West Ham FC forward), Steve Simpson (guitarist) and Keith Grant (drummer in "The Downliners"). Hayes was a tough working class area and quite a few of John's contemporaries graduated to join the upper echelons of London's criminal underworld.

Another kid who went to my school was called Eddie Richards... he went on to play the drums with "Edison Lighthouse". That Eddie still owes me a hundred quid from way back when... and I haven't forgotten it. (John Kerrison)

When John began attending Mellow Lane Comprehensive his father bought him his first bicycle, from "Rowleys" bike shop on the corner of Fairdale Gardens, to help him travel back and forth from home to school. It was manufactured by "Raleigh" and, as a result of strict import controls in force at that time, all of its robust components were entirely British made. This included a sprung leather saddle and the Sturmey-Archer three speed gear hub in the rear wheel. The maroon coloured cycle provoked a great deal of teasing from John's school chums because it was a very old-fashioned "sit up and beg" model with outdated push-rod brakes. When asked why he hadn't chosen a more modern racer style John would reply that his was a "proper" bike. It was a proper bike to John because his father had bought it for him.

The move to a new school required the purchase of the regulatory school uniform and Mrs Kerrison took John to Southall High Street because she preferred the shops there. At that time Southall did not have the dense Asian population for which it is so well known today. John recalls that there were only two children of Asian origin in the entire school at Mellow Lane Comprehensive and they both had the somewhat British surname of "Harris". The huge influx of immigrants from India and Pakistan didn't come about until the Woolf Rubber Works opened in Southall. The new factory created an enormous number of job vacancies which could not be filled by the local population, such was the employment situation in Prime

Minister Harold Macmillan's prosperous "never had it so good" late 1950s.

Another development which happened towards the end of that decade was the introduction of the 45 rpm single which rapidly began to replace the old-fashioned 78 rpm gramophone records. John had his own record player which, probably made by "Dansette", was blue and white with a lid and a built in speaker at the front. A control switch enabled it to play three speeds of record, 45 rpm and 78 rpm plus the new multitrack album format of $33^{1}/_{3}$ rpm. An auto-changer hook shaped arm allowed a sequence of eight singles to be played, dropping them one at a time onto the turntable from a stack. A far more sophisticated Philip's radiogram held pride of place in the front room. Although Mr Kerrison loved the combined radio and record player he would have much preferred to own a German manufactured "Blue Spot" radiogram, but he could not afford such an expensive high quality sound system. His favourite record was "Pennies from Heaven" sung by Bing Crosby. Another record that he played frequently was "Diana" by Paul Anka. John can also remember "Let There Be Drums" which was recorded by the legendary drummer Sandy Nelson.

The Kerrisons obtained their first television in around 1958 or 1959. It was set up high in an exalted position in the back room and was marvelled at by everyone who watched it. These days the black and white picture would be considered quite primitive but in its day it was thought to be state of the art. John's favourite programme was a Rock & Roll show called *"Oh Boy"* which was transmitted on Saturday. Another show called *"The Six Five Special"* was hosted by the ice cool and Brylcreem coiffured Pete Murray. One of the regular acts that John watched performing was a lady called Cherry Wainer who played a white Hammond organ. She was accompanied by a drummer called Don Storer who played on a "Trixon Speedfire" drum kit. John was completely mesmerised by the distinctive egg shaped bass drum which employed two sections and two bass pedals to produce contrasting sounds.

When I was a kid we didn't have a fridge, food was kept in the larder. My mother used to boil all the clothes and then squeeze them out in a mangle. I can remember when we got a Hoover Keymatic washing machine in the sixties. It had a small square of red plastic in a slot which selected the washing cycle. (John Kerrison)

When John was about 11 years old he went on a weekend camp with the Boy Scouts to a large sports event being held in Chigwell, Essex. In addition to the usual Scouting pursuits there was also football, cricket and golf. Amongst the attractions laid on at the Jamboree there was a teenage High School marching band from the USA and one of the instruments being played caught John's eye. It was a snare drum with the letters "WFL" written on it, denoting that it was made by the "William Frederick Ludwig" drum company. When John heard it being played he was inspired and hooked for life. He immediately made up his mind that he wanted to be a drummer, so much so that it became an obsession. After school he would attempt to construct an improvised drum kit made from old biscuit tins and other household items. Using wallpaper as a drum skin, held taut with elastic bands to form a snare drum, proved to be only partially successful. John begged his mother to buy him a real snare drum, like the one that he had seen in her Marshall Ward shopping catalogue "club book", he pleaded with her for almost a year.

His wish came true at Christmas time when he was given his first drum kit which comprised a sparkling red snare drum on a stand with a small bracket arm holding a single cymbal. It was called the "Kat Kit" and, made by Broadway Gigster, it came with a pair of basic hickory drumsticks plus a pair of drum-brushes. The purchase price of around nine pounds would have represented a considerable sum of money for John's parents to repay by weekly instalments. Whilst these days John disparagingly refers to the drum kit as being totally "Mickey Mouse" it is nevertheless quite obvious that receiving the Christmas present still remains a treasured memory. In a noise limitation exercise he was allowed to practise his percussion skills for one hour every evening upstairs in his sisters' bedroom. Kept warm by an old paraffin heater he drummed along to the songs on his record player. Despite his enthusiastic practice sessions John's first performance, playing along to records at a children's party, received little critical acclaim. One night his father returned home from working away and, perhaps after hearing his son's fledgling attempts to play, he announced that he was going to arrange for John to have drum lessons.

At that time there was a shop in Southall called "Seths" which sold electrical equipment including radios, radiograms and record players. Mr Kerrison always bought his records there and one day he saw a sign advertising drum lessons at fifteen shillings (seventy-five new pence) per hourly session. Unable to afford the tuition fee every week, he booked John to go once a fortnight. The teacher was the legendary Mr Jim Marshall, anyone who has ever gone to a Rock concert will almost certainly be familiar with the white italicised "Marshall" logo. In the 1960s and 1970s it was the most prevalent and instantly recognisable trade mark seen on the amplifiers and the awesome banks of loud speaker cabinets, stacked high upon the stage, in Rock venues all over the world. The Marshall sound system was worshipped by the devotees of Rock music and Jim Marshall himself became affectionately known amongst them as the "Lord of Loudness".

John took drum lessons for about eighteen months or so, first in Jim Marshall's home and then later in the Marshall music shop when it opened in Hanwell. At Jim's house the lessons took place in an ordinary room without any soundproofing. Students were taught using Jim Marshall's own four drum "Premier" kit which consisted of a bass drum, two tom-toms and a snare drum together with a crash cymbal plus a ride and hi-hat. In addition there was also a record player and a music stand. John learned the rudiments at first, such as how to hold the sticks in the "traditional" style; a technique originating from the military drummers who played a snare drum whilst marching on parade and into battle.

When teaching musical notation Jim Marshall would hand write the notes himself in a neat and precise manner typical of his background as a mechanical engineer. The tunes would usually be the dance hall music of those days such as Tangos, Waltzes and Quicksteps. Jim also taught other styles of drumming including Jazz, Rock & Roll and the Blues; the latter was always referred to as Rhythm & Blues at that time. One of the records played for John to accompany on the drums was "What Do You Want to Make Those Eyes at Me For?" by Emile Ford and The Checkmates. Another piece of practise material frequently employed in the lessons was Ravel's

"Bolero"; the continuously rising crescendo of the classical orchestral score provided quite a challenge for the budding percussionist. On the subject of learning rhythm and how to keep the beat, John firmly believes in that being something that you've either got or you haven't.

I was watching a drummer the other day, he was so wooden that he couldn't "swing" even if he had Albert Pierrepoint (the famous British hangman executioner) there to help him. (John Kerrison)

After a while the venue for drum lessons changed to a shop which Jim Marshall had opened on the Uxbridge Road in Hanwell. It was quite a small cramped retail space, probably no bigger than fifteen feet wide by twenty feet deep, stocked with an assortment of new and second hand instruments. There were Premier and Ludwig drums, several guitars, some Fender amplifiers, saxophones and lots of other musical paraphernalia. The shop soon became popular and many of the customers were youthful teenage novice musicians who would later achieve fame in the new genres of Rhythm & Blues and Rock & Roll. Although more than a decade had passed since the ending of hostilities certain items were still difficult to obtain in post war Britain, this included electronic amplifiers.

A lot of the drumming hardware was very inferior in those days, all of the screw threads would go because they were made of such poor metal. Everything used to work loose and fall apart. Keith Moon was known for wrapping a piece of rope around his drum kit to try and keep it together while he was smacking the hell out of it. (John Kerrison)

At the start of the 1960s musical tastes were changing away from the traditional Jazz and dance bands fronted by musicians playing instruments such as trumpets, clarinets and saxophones which needed little assistance in enabling them to be heard; the same unassisted audibility was also true for the drums. The new popular music increasingly being played in the dance halls and clubs pushed electric guitars to the fore and hence created a huge demand for sound amplification systems. Most of the successful bands performed using equipment such as the "Selmer Truvoice", the "Vox AC30", the "Watkins Dominator", the "Vortexian" or the rather expensive range manufactured by "Fender". There was also an echo chamber called the "Watkins Copicat" which employed looped recording tapes. Another excellent echo effect was produced using a magnetic recording disc in the "Binson Echorette".

However, for aspiring professionals and most amateur musicians such sophisticated sound systems were prohibitively priced and in very short supply due to import restrictions. Some guitarists attempted to overcome this obstacle by plugging into reel-to-reel tape recorders. Others resorted to crudely rewiring radios and record players, achieving varying degrees of success and incurring a grave danger to their personal safety from death by electrocution. In any event neither the professionally manufactured or the suicidally amateur amplifiers and speakers could produce the volume and the particular type of sound that the new wave of Rhythm & Blues guitarists really wanted.

Jim Marshall was a shrewd businessman and, having seen a lucrative marketing opportunity in the situation, he decided to sell his own brand of amplifiers and speakers. He teamed up with an electrical engineer and together they designed and built new sound systems in an out-building at the rear of the music shop. The loudness and the characteristic sound quality produced by the Marshall electronic equipment proved to be popular with musicians and, in order to increase production, the manufacturing side of the rapidly expanding business was moved first to a factory in Pump Lane in Hayes and from there to Bletchley. The Marshall trade mark soon began to achieve world wide success. The introduction of such high powered amplifiers on stage was not without consequences later in life for the Rock & Roll musicians who were the first to use them.

I have lost a bit of the hearing in my left ear from those days, a lot of the top frequencies have gone, which I put down mainly to the bass players... It only began to really show in later years. These days the guys in the bands usually wear earplugs as protection through which, with modern technology, they can still hear the sounds being played on a separate audio feed without relying on the speakers and risking any hearing damage. (John Kerrison)

Whilst the name Jim Marshall has achieved fame, for his contribution to the amplification of Rock music, John remembers his drumming mentor as a nice man who would often accept delayed payments for drum lessons or waive instalments on the purchase of musical instruments. Under his excellent tutelage and encouragement John soon progressed to a point where the Kat Kit snare drum was no longer adequate to practise on at home and his father agreed to get him a full professional drum kit. However, it was firmly stipulated that this was the last time that any equipment would be bought for John by his parents, in future he would have to buy his own drums.

People at that time used mainly British made kits such as Premier or Ajax and there was also stuff from a firm called Boosey and Hawkes. Trixon were German but not that brilliant. There was an embargo on all of the American gear until about 1957, even then they were hard to get hold of plus they were very expensive... only the top bands had them. (John Kerrison)

They purchased a second-hand drum kit from Jim Marshall's shop, financing the considerable monetary outlay by trading in the Kat Kit snare drum and paying off the outstanding balance by weekly instalments. The kit consisted of a Premier Black Pearl 20" x 14" bass drum with matching 12" x 8" and 16" x 20" tom-toms plus a Royal Ace 14" x 5.5" snare drum. In addition there was a full set of Zyn cymbals with a good quality Premier bass drum pedal and all the requisite stands. The bass drum and tom-toms had protective soft covers and there was also a "traps" case to transport the snare drum, cymbals, plus all the other hardware. Even with Jim Marshall's benevolent finance terms John's father could still not afford to buy all of the gear and so John agreed to sell his beloved Hornby train set, showing considerable commitment at such a young age towards fulfilling his ambition to be a drummer.

Chapter Seven

When I started gigging I didn't go for any more lessons with Jim Marshall because I was a cocky little git and I didn't think that I needed them... but I most definitely did. (John Kerrison)

On Saturday mornings John would usually cycle to Hanwell and hang around in Jim Marshall's shop on the Uxbridge Road. A number of musicians from various genres including Jazz, Rhythm & Blues and Rock & Roll would congregate there and chat amongst themselves about the music business. Some of them were seasoned professionals and they provided John with a great deal of useful anecdotal training in his chosen career. At regular intervals they would adjourn to Ted's cafe for a cup of tea with a cheese and tomato sandwich. Most of them were much older than John with the next youngest to him being at least two years his senior. People got a lot of work by hanging around in the shop, it was like an ad hoc job agency and several bands found new members and temporary replacements from recommendations provided by the shop's management and the clientele. However, the place would start to empty early in the afternoon because most of people there had a paying gig to go to on Saturday night.

As well as Ted's cafe there was another place near Jim Marshall's shop called "The Rendezvous"... it was a bit more upmarket... I couldn't afford the fish and chips that they did there. (John Kerrison)

Those regularly present at the shop included many of Jim Marshall's drum students and his son Terry Marshall who played the saxophone. John used to mix with several of the drummers who were taught by Jim Marshall including Terry Maybe, Terry Sealy, Mitch

Mitchell (who later played in the "Jimi Hendrix Experience") and Mick Underwood (who went on to play in bands such as the "Herd"). Some of the other Rock & Roll musicians learned to play music while serving in the post war Armed Forces, after being called up as teenagers to complete their obligatory two years of conscripted National Service. This included John's hero Carlo Little who played drums with "Screaming Lord Sutch and the Savages" and a nascent version of "The Rolling Stones". Carlo was well known for being a "big hitter" when it came to drumming style and it is no wonder that his protege Keith Moon (the irrepressible drummer for "The Who") later gained a similar reputation. Even when the dangerously eccentric "Moon the Loon" and the equally anarchic Screaming Lord Sutch were present in Jim Marshall's music shop the person causing most of the mayhem would usually be John Kerrison.

A drummer called Chris Sherwin worked in the music store, he was another pupil of Jim Marshall and he eventually became the shop manager. The sales assistant was a couple of years senior to John and kept an eye on the youngster, telling him off for horseplay such as chasing schoolgirls around the drum kits and instruments. One day Chris found that he had accidentally double booked himself and, having agreed to play at two different venues on the following Saturday, he gave John the opportunity to take one of the gigs off his hands. The fledgling percussionist jumped at the offer, he was about to turn professional at the tender age of thirteen.

There was a circuit of musicians in London and around the provinces where everybody knew everybody. The drummers that I met in Jim Marshall's shop would keep on replacing each other in different bands and so our paths would keep crossing all the time as we all shuffled around. (John Kerrison)

John's first paid public performance was at a dance in a sports and social club next to the landmark art deco Hoover factory in Perivale, his father drove him there and picked him up afterwards. The rest of the band were all young men aged from eighteen to twenty-five and John was very nervous. Furthermore the music was "Trad" Jazz and, unaccustomed to the quick tempo, John had great difficulty in keeping up. He kept his head down and managed to finish the gig without too many major musical disasters.

Afterwards the guy said to me "You'll never make it as a drummer". But he still paid me my thirty bob (£1.50) and that inspired me more than anything to carry on practising. (John Kerrison)

Subsequently John got a phone call, made following a recommendation by someone in the Marshall music shop, inviting him to join a band from Greenford called "The Cossacks". Their manager was a Mr Lewis who drove a great big flashy American Studebaker car and, by all accounts, was a bit of a colourful character. It was said that he had apparently "come into some money" which enabled him to finance The Cossacks for the benefit of his sons, Keith Lewis was the lead singer and guitarist whilst his brother Mervin Lewis played the bass guitar. There was also another band member, who was not related to the others, on rhythm guitar.

Attending practice sessions with the band in Greenford presented a daunting logistical problem for John when his father was working away from home, until the ever reliable Mrs Kerrison came to the rescue. Whilst John would carry his traps case the half mile or so walk from his house to the bus stop she would accompany him, pushing her bicycle along with the cumbersome bass drum resting on the step-through between the handle bars and the saddle. The tom-toms were too much extra baggage and John went to the rehearsals without them. Once he got on the bus he was on his own and when he got off the bus in Greenford he had to carry his kit for about two hundred and fifty yards unaided. It all took a great deal of effort, but John was determined to fulfil his ambition to be a drummer. Fortunately he always got a lift home after rehearsals and gigs.

In the 50s and 60s some of the Jazz drummers used to have an 18 or 20 inch bass drum and a 14 inch floor tom plus a really thin snare drum. It was less kit to hump around from gig to gig. It kind of set a trend as a type of Jazz kit. (John Kerrison)

51

The Cossacks used to play mostly at local venues such as the British Legion and the Monday Club which was held at the St Christopher Youth Club near the Cuckoo Lane Estate in Greenford. The band employed an amplifier which was rather primitive compared to the models which became available later. Their repertoire consisted mainly of the popular hits by American Rock & Roll performers such as Chuck Berry, Bruce Channel, Elvis Presley, Gene Vincent as well as some British singers including Cliff Richard. One evening a man who used to hang around the band offered to give John a lift home after a gig. However, the apparently well intentioned benefactor turned out to be a predatory paedophile. Luckily John managed to escape and run away unharmed. He never told his parents about the incident, probably in case they panicked and decided not to allow him to continue playing anymore gigs. Nevertheless, from that day on, he was quite wary of strangers.

John didn't earn much money out of drumming for the group but he did gain a great deal of valuable experience. In the summer of 1961 The Cossacks entered the "Battle of the bands" competition at the annual Hayes and Harlington pop festival which was held in Hayes Park and, up against some stiff competition, they came first. They played in front of an enthusiastic crowd of teenagers who were dancing around the bandstand. Their victory was actually not that surprising, John was a local boy and the audience was packed out with many of his school friends and family relatives who turned up to vote for him. There was no cash prize but it must have provided John with great kudos, especially amongst his peers and mentors in Jim Marshall's music shop.

We were a bit structured in those days, it was the way I was taught, there were rules. Then I learned that there are no rules and I did my own thing. Moony had a different way of playing, it was different to everyone else... it was his concept of where it was. (John Kerrison)

Every summer the Lewis family used to go on holiday to Jaywick Sands, near the Essex town of Clacton-on-sea, where they had a timber built chalet. One year John accompanied them when they took the whole band, complete with their instruments and gear. Some of the band were given a lift in a Ford Zephyr owned by a man called Bill Dunton, at one point the car reached one hundred miles per hour which impressed John and his friends. Mr Lewis had the novel idea of promoting The Cossacks by getting them to set up their equipment on the beach and play to an audience of holiday makers. They didn't obtain any official permission for their spur of the moment performance, in those days no one bothered about such trivial matters. Their sound system was plugged into a borrowed electricity supply and they just got on with it.

John ended up playing with The Cossacks for about a year before moving on and joining a band called "Paul and the Alpines". The line-up was Paul Lonergan on vocals with Dave Dove on bass guitar and Ray Kirkham playing lead guitar. Alfie Fripp was the rhythm guitarist, his father ran the dance hall in Wistowe House. In fact everybody in the band lived in the Hayes locality so it was very easy for them to get together to rehearse in their front rooms or at the nearby Pinkwell Youth Club. They often learned the chords and the arrangements of popular tunes by listening to records. The band kept changing the sound systems that they used, experimenting with a Meazzi PA followed by a Marshall PA plus Watkins Dominators and some of the other makes of equipment available at that time.

The Alpines went to an audition at Hammersmith arranged by the Roy Tempest Agency, a legendary show business promotion organisation in the "swinging" 1960s, who were based in London's trendy West End. There were around eight bands all set up to play in a little room and each group had to perform three numbers. The boys from Hayes played really well and greatly impressed impressario Roy Tempest. At that time the age of majority when a child legally becomes an adult was still twenty-one years of age, a statutory definition which was not lowered to eighteen until 1970. This meant that John's father had to sign the contract on his son's behalf. Mr Kerrison and the other fathers were just ordinary working men and they had no real understanding as to what they were signing. On the way home John took out a packet of Peter Stuyvesant cigarettes and offered one to his father, it was the first time that he had ever smoked in front of his dad.

Shortly after signing to the Roy Tempest Agency bookings for the band began pouring in. A man called Sid Foreman, John's next door neighbour in Botwell Common Road, became their manager for a while; he was about nineteen years old and provided transport to the gigs. Paul Lonergan, the lead singer, was around eighteen years old whilst the rest of the band were only fifteen. They played at a lot of the pubs and the dance halls in and around London and, as most of them were under eighteen, they were lucky to have been allowed to perform in those venues which were licensed premises. Many of the gigs were in places such as church halls which were let out in order to raise funds and there would rarely be any alcohol on sale, just crisps and lemonade. John never developed a taste for the popular fizzy cola drinks, introduced from the USA along with the Rhythm & Blues music, and he usually drank tea or water.

The band played at lot of the US military bases scattered all around the country including West Ruislip, Upper Heyford, Mildenhall, Lakenheath and Brize Norton; effectively playing "their own music" back to the American servicemen. Performing at the bases was like visiting a foreign country in that money had to be changed into US dollars in order to buy drinks in the bar. John liked visiting the "PX store" to purchase items imported from the USA which were not available elsewhere. The next day he would show off at school by offering his friends a Pall Mall cigarette or a bottle of Budweiser beer, despite being too young to legally consume either of such contraband items.

Paul and the Alpines were regularly booked to play at the Ryde Hotel on the Isle of Wight where they would stay overnight and return home the next morning. That winter the snow was thick on the ground and, as a consequence of the inclement weather, they were not allowed to take their van on the ferry to get to the gig. Undaunted the band commandeered a British Rail baggage trolley and piled all of their gear on to it. After crossing the Solent they arrived in Ryde and then pushed the heavily laden truck all the way up the hill to the hotel. Also in that winter the van's engine seized up when they were travelling home from a gig in Crawley and they were stuck overnight in the freezing cold. John and the rest of the band kept crossing the road to an all night petrol station in order to obtain numerous cups of vile tasting but warming hot tea from a vending machine. When the morning came they were finally rescued by relatives.

In Crawley the band often used to play up above a Burton's tailor shop. Another regular venue for the Alpines was the "Assembly Rooms" in Walthamstow where there were three bands playing every Saturday night. A frequent booking much nearer home, practically on John's doorstep, was Wistowe House; possibly aided by the fact that rhythm guitarist Alf Fripp's father ran the dance hall there. Steve Priest, a fellow pupil of John's from Mellow Lane Comprehensive School, regularly played bass guitar there with a band called "The Countdowns".

Another resident band at Wistowe House was "Ronnie and the High Tones". The lead singer Ronnie, who lived just down the road from John, got sacked by his group and they went looking for a better vocalist. Somehow they got hold of Ian Gillan (who later became the front man for "Deep Purple") and changed their name to the "Javelins". John recalls that Ian actually wanted to call the band "Jess Gillan and the Javelins" but, for some reason or another, that never happened. He became good friends with Ian who, at about seventeen years of age, was two years older than the schoolboy drummer. The rest of The Javelins line-up comprised Gordon Fairminer on guitar, Keith Roach on drums, Tony Tacon on lead guitar and Tony Whitfield on bass guitar.

The Alpines and the Javelins played alternate Thursdays at Wistowe House and John played with them a couple of times, standing in when their drummer Keith Roach wasn't available. The Alpines and the Javelins had a very similar play list including songs recorded by Eddie Cochran, Buddy Holly, Elvis Presley and Gene Vincent. John's band also covered "In the Hall of the Mountain King" by Nero and the Gladiators, "Hey Baby" by Bruce Channel, and "Great Balls of Fire" by Jerry Lee Lewis.

I met him (Ian Gillan) at Wistowe House and we hit it off straight away because we were both into Rock & Roll and we both smoked cigarettes. He had the looks, he was a total magnet for girls, and he had an enormous vocal range. There was also something else about him and, whatever it was, he was always going to be a star. (John Kerrison)

The Alpines were soon gaining experience and improving their stage craft, as they performed gig after gig, developing a more "sophisticated" act. As a finale Paul the singer would go backstage and take his trousers off before coming back on wearing nothing but a grass hula-hula skirt. He would then sing "Good Golly Miss Molly" and, with his modesty protected by a black posing pouch, he would dance provocatively gyrating his hips to an appreciative female audience. It was pure showmanship and very classy stuff. Blond haired Paul was a handsome young man with plenty of fans amongst the ladies.

One night, when The Alpines were playing at the Assembly Rooms in Walthamstow, we had to wait ages before we could start packing the gear away after the gig. Paul was entertaining a young lady in the back of the van which was mysteriously rocking up and down. (John Kerrison)

Many of the venues still had a revolving mirror ball suspended from the ceiling, a vestige from the days when they hosted ballroom dances. The new audiences for Rock & Roll bands were composed almost entirely of teenage kids. All the girls would prance around their handbags, moving in time to the music, while the boys watched and plucked up the courage to ask them for a dance. Some of the younger teenage girls dressed as "Bobby Soxers" whilst their older counterparts dressed in big skirts with multiple layers of petticoats. Spinning around on the dance floor the young ladies would occasionally show a flash of bare skin above a nylon stocking top, a sight which left an indelible impression on an adolescent John Kerrison.

When the 1950s turned into the 1960s there was a distinct change in fashion and practically everything else. Post war prosperity brought about an increase in the average disposable income which was particularly noticeable in the nation's youth. The Jazz loving peaceful Beatniks and their counterpart fractious Teddy-boys started to face near extinction as they began to be replaced by youth cultures such as the Mods and the Rockers. The development of the distinctive tribal cults was driven by the anthems from Rock & Roll and Rhythm & Blues played on the juke box. The burgeoning teenage Mod obsession for smart stylish clothes drew a great deal of inspiration from America and Italy in particular. Popping amphetamine pills, such as the triangular "purple hearts", gave the teenagers the energy to party all night as they danced to their favourite R & B music.

John enthusiastically joined the ranks of the Mods at fifteen when his father bought him a brown suit from Burtons. The so called "bum freezer" jacket was tailored with a box back and the trousers were cut in the straight legged "drainpipe" style. A pair of fashionable Italian side laced winkle-picker shoes completed John's chic ensemble. However, the young drummer didn't really mix much with the local Mods who used to congregate in and around the Wimpy Bar in Hayes. Playing at gigs left little time for John to socialise with his fellow devotees of Mod culture, besides which he was still not old enough to ride a motor scooter.

The Alpines were a popular band amongst the Mods in West London and they got plenty of bookings. John usually got paid between three and five pounds as his "divi" share from each of the gigs that they played, his school friends considered him to be a "Mr Moneybags" because he always had cash in his pockets. He could afford to buy fashionable clothes from a shop in Hayes called "Mr Howard's". Everyone wore Levi jeans but John preferred to wear Lee jeans just to be different. Every week he usually bought around three records in order to keep up to date with the latest hits and to practice the drum techniques of successful drummers.

Chapter Eight

"I quit school at fifteen... The headmaster said choose academia
or Rock & Roll... I chose Rock & Roll. (John Kerrison)

In the summer of 1962 John again took part in the "Battle of the Bands" which was held in Hayes Park and his group won for the second year in a row. On this occasion he was drumming with Paul and the Alpines but still employed the same tactics, packing the audience with friends and family, as he had done with The Cossacks the previous year. John reached the minimum school leaving age of fifteen in August, a decade later it was raised to sixteen, but he voluntarily stayed on at Mellow Lane Comprehensive School and joined the fifth form. However, with three or four gigs a week he often got home late and was too tired to get up in time for school the next morning.

Going to watch Hayes FC play on a Saturday also became a thing of the past because there was always a booking to travel to with the band. John played in goal for the school team and helped them win a competition semi-final only to be dropped for the final, which was just as well because he had a gig to go to that evening. After just one term in the fifth form John left school and, although there were plans for him to go to night school, he ended up with just one RSA in Technical Drawing. Despite this his parents still gave their son's ambition to be a drummer their utmost support. Returning home at four in the morning after a gig he would always find that his mother had left out a flask of tea with a plate of sandwiches and that she had turned on the electric blanket to warm his bed.

John also discovered another benefit from playing in a band in the shape of his first real girlfriend, a young lady called Jean Coupleditch. She was a little older than John but she was impressed by his smart Mod style suit and his drumming skills when she saw him playing with The Casuals at the Havelock Youth Club. He would catch the 195 bus over to Southall to meet her and then go courting in Osterley Park. However, he found it very difficult to play with the band four or five nights a week whilst dating Jean at the same time.

One Sunday, when I was on my way to catch the 195 bus, a guy hanging out of a white Commer van shouted "Oi mate, where's Botwell House?" and I told him that he was parked right in front of it. Then I realised that he was Joe Brown, he was a top pop star in those days... all the top acts played at Botwell House. (John Kerrison)

John was still drumming with Paul and the Alpines when he started work as an apprentice with a large engineering company in Southall called AEC who were later taken over by Leyland, the firm manufactured buses including the famous "Routemaster" double-decker. Having become a "working man" he marked the occasion by ordering a brand new drum kit to replace the second hand equipment which had been bought for him by his father. Jim Marshall's music shop supplied him with a full Premier kit in a silver sparkle finish comprising of a 22" x 16" bass drum, a 14" x 8" tom-tom, a 16" x 16" floor tom-tom, a 17" K Zildjian crash cymbal, a 20" Avedis Zildjian ride cymbal plus a pair of 15" Avedis Zildjian high hats. To cap it all there was a special snare drum, a Ludwig 400, the very same model played by the legendary Jazz drummer Joe Morello from the "Dave Brubeck Quartet"; it is a drum which John still owns and treasures today.

This time John, as previously stipulated by his parents, had to find the money himself and so he bought the drums on credit. The repayments were thirty shillings (£1.50) a week and, after he paid his mother the same amount for his keep, he was left with just one shilling (5p) to live on from his weekly take-home pay of three pounds and a shilling. However, he could still rely on the extra income which he received from playing the drums and so he always had plenty of cash in his pockets.

The snare drum alone cost thirty-nine guineas (£40.95p) and when I went to pick it up from Jim Marshall's shop one of my other drumming heroes called Micky Burt was there. "That's an awful lot of money to pay for a snare drum," he said, but I didn't care. I thought that if Joe Morello can play one then so can I... In those days I really was that cocky. (John Kerrison)

Soon after he started work at AEC his relationship with the band began to sour. He already suspected that the Roy Tempest Agency was double dealing with their appearance fees. Sometimes at a venue the band would be paid directly from the takings instead of the money being sent to the Roy Tempest Agency. The agreed payment would often be thirty pounds instead of the fifteen or twenty pounds that they normally received before deduction of the agent's ten percent. There was also disagreement within the band as to how the gig money should be split. John felt that everyone in the band was getting new gear bought for them whereas he was paying the instalments on his drum kit out of his own pocket.

When the band spent a great deal of money on a new PA system without consulting John it brought matters to a head, especially as the drum kit was never "miked up" in those days. John threatened to quit and insisted on receiving a special snare drum stand which cost twelve pounds. After much moaning from the rest of the band they agreed to his demand. However, at the very next gig John again got what he thought was less than a full share of the appearance money and he made up his mind that it was time to move on. Although he was still only fifteen John was determined to fulfil his ambition of becoming a drummer in a top band.

The last gig that John played with Paul and the Alpines was in early 1963 at a place called "Botwell House" in Hayes town. It was part of the rebuilt Roman Catholic "Immaculate Heart of Mary" church and the venue was run by an American Priest called Father Gamm; in order to raise parochial funds he used to put on a dance nearly every night of the week. Just about every top band played there including Cliff Bennett and the Rebel Rousers, The Rolling Stones, Screaming Lord Sutch and the Savages, Joe Brown and the Brothers, Peter Jay and the Jaywalkers, Nero and the Gladiators, plus many others. Practically the only famous band that didn't perform at Botwell house was The Beatles.

In 1961 Father Gamm organised one of the first open air pop festivals ever held in the UK. It was in the grounds of Botwell House and Del Shannon came over from the USA... there was another festival held the following year. (John Kerrison)

One evening John and his friends went to see a band called "Frankie Reid and the Casuals" who were performing at Botwell House. John deliberately attempted to annoy the group by messing around in front of the stage and chatting up all of their girlfriends. The audience was a little sparse that evening and the band couldn't fail to be aware of his antics.

I got a telephone call inviting me to do an audition at the Viaduct pub in Hanwell for Frankie Reid and the Casuals. They instantly recognised me as the cocky little git who was trying to pull their girlfriends when they played at Botwell House. Anyway, they must've liked what I did because I still got the job. (John Kerrison)

At sixteen years old John was the youngest member of Frankie Reid and the Casuals, the rest of the band were all well over sixteen and consisted of Frankie Reid on lead vocals, Ian Holland on lead guitar, Chris Jackson on rhythm guitar and Steve Hargreaves on bass. One of the first venues that the new line-up played was Ealing Town Hall. John found himself following in the footsteps of drummers Terry Maybe, Terry Sealy and Mitch Mitchell, some of his fellow students from Jim Marshall's music shop, all of whom had previously played in The Casuals. The band was managed by Bill Dunton who had sold his Ford Zephyr and drove a Dormobile with "Frankie Reid and the Casuals" painted on each side, he later moved on to a white Commer van.

The girls used to write on the van after the gig in those days. We would go around with loads of names written in the dirt, scratched into the paintwork or spelled out in lipstick... all done by the female fans who liked us. (John Kerrison)

Bill was a nice man and he was fairly open about being gay, a candidness which was rather dangerous at that time because violent "queer-bashing" homophobia was rife and homosexuality wasn't legalised until 1967. Bill used to promote the band, find gigs and drive the van to the venues. He and the five band members all took an equal share of the gig money which was a good deal because he also paid for the petrol and other outgoings from of his sixth of the takings. Joining Frankie Reid and the Casuals was a step up for John and the money was very good, usually about five pounds a gig. He was always flush with money, whereas his friends were habitually skint, especially as he was still living at home and also getting paid whilst working at AEC.

All the apprentices at AEC had to first work for quite some time as an office boy before they were sent to learn the required engineering skills. Not only did John hate the boring clerical work but he was also horrified to discover that his wages would actually go down when he was sent to the training school. After about six months at AEC he gave in his notice and left. His friend Myles Lee was working at the Imperial College sports ground over in Harlington, where Chelsea FC used to train, and he got John a job there. The wages were six pounds a week and the duties included mowing the grass on the four football pitches and the four rugby pitches. John was also expected to work in the bar during busy periods which, because he would often be absent at a gig, soon brought him into conflict with Arthur the sports ground manager.

We didn't have that much gear and so there was plenty of room in the van. Travelling home at night the band used to pull down my trousers and push me up against one of the back windows so that the drivers following behind would see my backside in their headlights. (John Kerrison)

Frankie Reid and the Casuals played at a large number of venues all over south-east England from Northampton down to the south-coast including Gosport, Southampton and Waterlooville plus much of London from Ealing to Peckham. They travelled everywhere in a flat nosed Commer van which had no heating, wearing Army surplus sleeping bags to keep warm when they journeyed home late in the evening. The band got hold of a couple of old coach seats from somewhere and installed them in the back of the van to make it more comfortable. John made use of the seats when, at sixteen years old, he lost his virginity to a singularly unattractive mature lady at a gig in Egham. Afterwards he ran into the dressing room to inform band members Chris Jackson and Steve Hargreaves of his conquest. They told him that he should immediately wash himself in the sink to prevent catching something dangerously infectious. Both Chris and Steve were both over twenty-one years old and John naively took their advice without question, he didn't realise that they were making fun of him until he heard them screaming with laughter behind his back.

I wasn't confident with women, especially with ladies that I didn't know. I was much more confident behind the drum kit than anywhere else. They always say that we had loads of women, but I didn't have loads of women, I had a few but I didn't have that many. There were quite a few groupies around but they always used to go for the singer... it was the singer or the guitar players. (John Kerrison)

Not long after John turned sixteen he acquired a motor scooter, the ultimate Mod accoutrement. It was a blue and white Lambretta GT 200 which he bought brand new from Rowleys in Hayes on a hire purchase agreement, the same shop which supplied his first bicycle; Rowleys also had a record shop in a parade on Coldharbour Lane. John passed his test first time and he soon set about customising the machine to his own taste. The scooter was resprayed midnight blue and fitted with chrome panels, a chrome front wheel mudguard, chrome crash bars and a backrest which held a spare wheel. A stolen Mercedes symbol was also bolted to the bodywork as an anti establishment gesture. John would have preferred the prestigious bonnet mascot from a Jaguar, or a "Spirit of Ecstasy" from off a Rolls Royce, but his attempts to free one from its tenacious mounting proved unsuccessful.

Scooters were notoriously dangerous, the small wheels had a tendency to skid on white road markings or drain covers and unseat the rider. Furthermore, a scooter was of no use for transporting John's drum kit to a gig; but it had style and that was the important thing. The main drawback for Mods was the exposed riding position which, in bad weather, could result in ruin for their smart tailored suits. A solution was found in the "Parka", a drab sage green three quarter length hooded anorak which was worn as a protective coverall. The ex US military issue coats were cheap and in plentiful supply at the Army surplus stores following the Korean War. Parkas soon became another iconic item of Mod fashion and were often adorned with badges, RAF roundels or the masculine symbol for the Roman god Mars. There was no legal requirement to wear a crash helmet when riding a scooter or a motorcycle and John, forsaking safety for style, preferred the negligible head protection offered by a smart flat cap.

John used to ride over to Peckham Rye to see Reg Bodman, the bass player in Frankie Reid and the Casuals. Reg also had a scooter, a Vespa 180, and the pair of Mods often went to see a few bands play when The Casuals weren't gigging. There was actually very little of the brutal Mod versus Rocker gang warfare reported in the newspapers; the Mods were too worried about spoiling their expensive clothes and the Rockers, also referred to as "Greasers", were more interested in achieving the 100 mph "ton-up" on their customised and highly tuned cafe racer motorbikes. John's cousin Alan Kerrison was a Rocker and he had a powerful Triumph Bonneville T120 650cc motorcycle. He took John for a ride and scared him stiff, scooters were all about style and not speed.

Frankie Reid and the Casuals played covers of songs that were in the pop charts by acts like Elvis, Chuck Berry, James Brown and even female groups such as the "The Ronnettes". They tried to copy and emulate all of the popular hits of the day whilst, at the same time, adding something of their own musical interpretation and style. The band worked really hard and gained quite a following, especially around West London. Sometimes they were on the same bill, or even the support band, playing with many big name bands of that era. This included "The Roulettes" who, playing as Adam Faith's backing band, recorded several hit songs. In the sixties there were an awful lot of live music venues in and around London, many more than there are today; at one time or another John played at most of them.

There was a club in Ladbroke Grove, operating in a basement below a shop, which had a large West Indian clientele but the preferred music was still Rock & Roll. One very unusual venue was the "Silver Blades" ice rink in Streatham, the bands played on one side whilst everyone danced around skating on the ice. A club in Uxbridge was called "Burtons" because it was above a tailor's which was part of the Burton chain of men's clothing shops. The "Blue Moon" was held in the social club at Hayes FC. Most of the really big name bands played at the Southall Community Centre. In addition there were several other pubs and clubs which provided a venue for live music.

In between his own gigs John sometimes managed to see bands such as "Cliff Bennett and the Rebel Rousers", "The Animals" and "The Graham Bond Organisation". Watching the top acts perform on stage fuelled his ambition and greatly influenced him as he developed his own style as a drummer. Screaming Lord Sutch and his band "The Savages" often played at the Blue Moon, the line-up included Carlo Little who was one of John's drumming heroes.

Sutchy used to do mad things like sing from inside a coffin or do "I'm A Hog For You Baby" with a toilet seat hung around his neck... he once climbed up into the metal rafters while singing. He had some of those great big tins that they kept crisps in when they were still sold in grease proof paper bags... he used to set the tins alight and sing "Great Balls of Fire". (John Kerrison)

However, the definitive showman of that era was undoubtably Johnny Kidd with his band "The Pirates". John saw them when they played at the Southall Community Centre and was very impressed by their style and raw energy. At that time the line-up comprised Johnny Kidd on lead vocals, Micky Green on lead guitar, Johnny Spence on bass guitar and Frank Farley on drums. Johnny Kidd had a number one chart hit with "Shakin' all over" which he wrote himself. The classic Rock & Roll song includes a short but memorable drum break, just before the guitar solo, which practically every drummer on the planet has practised at some point. The band recorded several other hit songs and attracted a huge number of screaming female fans plus all the fame and fortune associated with such success. The Pirates were everything that John had dreamed of being a part of since he was twelve years old.

Chapter Nine

It was 1964, that's when I bought a James Brown record called "Out of Sight". The drummer was Melvin Parker, he was a revelation to me because of his syncopated bass drum rhythms... I knew that this was the way to go. (John Kerrison)

The Ealing Jazz Club was in a basement under the ABC Bakery opposite Ealing Broadway Tube station. It was run by a man who went by the name of "Ferry", who John thinks was of Arabic origin, along with Alexis Corner and a well respected harmonica player called Cyril Davies. The venue had originally gained a reputation for its Blues music until Rock & Roll took over. Inside it was subterranean dark and the dampness caused those in contact with the PA systems much concern about the lethal powers of electricity. Many world famous musicians and bands played there including a fledgling version of The Rolling Stones. Prior to gaining worldwide fame The Stones' original line-up held the resident band spot at the club on Thursday nights, until the booking was taken over by Frankie Read and the Casuals.

One night after a gig at the Ealing Jazz Club I went to the Wimpy Bar in West Ealing with the rest of the band. The Who walked in and we had a fight throwing bread rolls. (John Kerrison)

When The Casuals were playing at the Ealing Jazz Club Keith Moon would often ask if he could have a go on the drums, John would agree and take the opportunity to go outside for a cigarette break.

Moony was a little short-arse but he was a big hitter even before he started getting all raucous and kicking the kit over when he

66

played with The Who. I could hit them hard but not like him and I used to worry about him breaking my drum kit, but he never ever did. I've still got the snare drum that he played on. (John Kerrison)

Botwell House was very much on John's home turf and he played the venue many times with several different bands. The Rolling Stones performed there in 1963 shortly after releasing their first record which was a cover of Chuck Berry's "Come On". The Casuals were the support band that evening and John did not rate Mick Jagger and his group that highly, they were good but by no means brilliant. However, in a short while The Rolling Stones achieved international stardom and the teenage music lovers at that time split into two camps. There were those who followed The Stones' rebellious bad boy image as opposed to those who preferred the clean cut angelic goodness of The Beatles. John was most definitely in the camp for The Rolling Stones.

It is very much a worn out old cliché to say that everyone remembers where they were on Friday 22 November 1963 when they heard the news that the American President "JFK" John Kennedy had been assassinated in Dallas Texas. John remembers the day because he was playing at the Kingsbury Grammar School in Honeypot Lane with Frankie Reid and the Casuals. The Beachcombers were also on the bill and Keith Moon was their drummer at that time.

I was coming off the stage when Moony runs down the corridor towards me shouting "John, John, the Russians have just shot Kennedy". Then he went on and played with The Beachcombers. (John Kerrison)

Around a year or so after John had joined Frankie Reid and the Casuals, sometime towards the end of 1964, the band underwent a drastic transformation. The lead vocalist Frank bought a dark blue Commer van and, now that he was able to transport the group himself, he decided that they didn't need a manager anymore; consequently Bill Dunton got the sack. There was also a change in the line-up when bass player Steve Hargreaves was replaced by Reg Bodman and then Mickey Lieber took over as lead guitarist from Ian

67

Holland. Later Mike Lieber played with the band "Python Lee Jackson" on their hit "In a Broken Dream" sung by Rod Stewart, he found further chart success with "Ashton Gardner and Dyke" who had a hit with "Resurrection Shuffle". Around Christmas 1964 The Casuals started to struggle for all sorts of reasons and then Frank announced that his wife was pregnant, making him unsure whether he could continue being away from home gigging several nights a week. After a short while the band demised.

A group called "The Rockin' Eccentrics" telephoned John and asked him if he would stand in as their drummer, they had been booked to play a Sunday lunchtime gig at the Greenford Hotel on the Uxbridge Road; a venue which has since become a MacDonald's. The band liked John's drumming style and they asked him to join them on a permanent basis. The line-up was Bruce Watts on rhythm guitar, Mick Liddell on lead vocals, Roy Robinson on bass guitar and Peter Maggs on lead guitar. It was a very successful combination and their gigs soon started to attract a large number of enthusiastically loyal fans. The band worked hard for quite some time before attracting the attention of an agency, based in offices at Jermyn Street London SW1, called Ashley Sinclair Enterprises Ltd. Following a successful audition The Rockin' Eccentrics were signed up by the prestigious music promotion company.

When John met Messrs Ashley and Sinclair he was very impressed. They both wore expensive silk suits and, a cause of great fascination to the band, near transparent silk socks; it was obvious that they were two guys with money. The businessmen had ambitious plans for The Rockin' Eccentrics, around Easter 1965 they shortened the name to "The Eccentrics" and signed a recording contract with PYE Records. Subsequently the band were booked into a small recording studio in Dean Street which, situated in the infamous Soho area of London's West End, was surrounded by strip clubs and seedy sex shows. John and his colleagues had to carry all of their equipment, including the amplifiers and drums, up three flights of stairs. It was hard work for the teenagers and they were not helped by the group of scantily clad women who, standing outside the next door topless bar, made suggestive comments in an attempt to embarrass the young men.

The Eccentrics were extremely impressed by the array of "space age" electronic equipment in the Dean Street studio. There was a two track recording system which was very primitive by todays standards, modern recording studios now employ an unlimited number of computerised mixable channels. In the 1960s they overcame the limitations imposed by having only two recording tracks by "bouncing" one track onto another, starting with the backing track and then building layer upon layer to form the complete song. There was a drawback inherent in this system in that each bounce resulted in a small reduction in quality, this was a feature which contributed to the characteristic sound of many Rock & Roll singles from that era. The band recorded a song written by the writing duo Carol King and Gerry Goffin called "What you got". A track penned by a man called Spiro with the dubious title of "Fe Fi Fo Fum" was recorded for the B side. The 45 rpm single was released on the PYE label (Catalogue No. 7N.15850) but failed to achieve any major chart success. These days The Eccentrics' one and only record release has become a valuable collector's item.

Ashley and Sinclair attempted to give The Eccentrics a "clean cut" image by changing their look and all the band members were sent to a tailor to be measured up for identical suits in a blue mohair material. The suit trousers were straight legged and the jackets had three buttons with two "bum flap" vents at the rear. Their new ensemble, paid for by the agency, was completed by thin black ties and plain white shirts. The drastic sartorial transformation was recorded in a publicity photo which appeared in the local "County Times and Gazette" newspaper on Friday 7 May 1965, the picture was accompanied by an article claiming that the scruffy look was no longer in vogue.

Shortly afterwards Ashley and Sinclair succeeded in getting The Eccentrics a slot in an audition which was held at a venue called the "Ad Lib Club". The prestigious night club was located above the Prince Charles Theatre in Leicester Place and it was very much the "in" venue where many of the rich and famous personalities, from the world of pop music and show business, went to "see and be seen". John recalls that the "Moody Blues" were sitting in the audience and he later bumped into a singer from the "Hollies" in the lift. There were around twenty bands competing for the prize of being the first British group to be booked to play a month long residency at the famous "*Il Piper*" club in Rome. The Eccentrics played really well and won the competition. A band called "The Bad Boys" from Northolt, who were friends of John's, claimed the second spot and they were booked to play in Rome after The Eccentrics finished their stint.

The drummer in The Bad Boys was called Tex… he told me that I was the first person he had ever seen play the syncopated rhythm. (John Kerrison)

John was still working at the Imperial College sports ground and gave in his notice when he knew that he was going to Italy. He got a temporary job through a friend working for Wimpey in a civil engineering yard as a labourer, John hated the boring drudgery but it filled in time while he waited to set off across Europe with the band. In preparation for the gig in Italy a large canvas banner was commissioned by Ashley and Sinclair to advertise the group.

I went to Italy in 1965 and discovered what they call there "La dolce vita"… the good life… I really loved it. (John Kerrison)

The five band members crammed their gear into a Ford van and set off to Dover where they caught the cross channel ferry to Calais. As they drove through France and part of Belgium the continental toilets, consisting of a hole with two footplates, came as something of a culture shock. That evening they arrived in North Germany and stayed the night in a Bed and Breakfast hotel in a town called "Ulm"situated on the banks of the River Danube. They ate in the downstairs bar where the owner entertained them by performing a dance like a chicken and pretending to "lay" boiled eggs. Foreign travel was proving to be an altogether bizarre experience for the young men, especially as none of them had ever travelled overseas before.

The van's alternator had broken down on route to Ulm but, despite the language barrier, the next morning they managed to get it repaired fairly easily; Ford motor parts are usually somewhat universal in availability. After successfully navigating their way to

Rome without any major problems the band located the Piper club in the Via Tagliamento before settling into the hotel Villa Norma in the Via Oglio. They were about to congratulate themselves when they discovered some rather large problems which they had failed to anticipate. Firstly they quickly realised that their large publicity banner was in English, nobody had taken into account the fact that it would be mostly unintelligible to the vast majority of Italians who spoke only their native tongue. It was a small particular which rendered the banner practically useless and a needless waste of valuable space in the van.

Furthermore, The Eccentrics' amplifiers and other electrical equipment was only compatible with the British 240 volt AC system. The band were horrified when they discovered that the Italian electricity supply was a completely different voltage, the situation looked completely hopeless. Fortunately the two men who ran the Piper club introduced the band to an English girl who spoke fluent Italian and, with the invaluable assistance provided by the bilingual young lady, they managed to buy a voltage converting transformer which saved the day.

John and his teenaged associates found Italy to be a strange place compared to their own homeland and the Italians thought the same of their British visitors. A couple of the musicians had longish "pudding basin" haircuts and, as the band walked down the street towards their hotel, the locals stared at them as if they were aliens from another planet. John witnessed a road accident when a driver, distracted by the sight of the British band, crashed into the back of another car. Prior to the United Kingdom joining the European Union there was no cross border employment mobility and The Eccentrics had to apply for work permits at the local police station. Nobody noticed that John was under eighteen and he, together with the rest of the group, were issued with the requisite employment visas.

One of the managers at the Piper club was called Giancarlo Bornigia… he took the band on a sightseeing tour around Rome in an open top Mercedes car… We felt special. (John Kerrison)

The Piper Club was the most famous club in Italy and it is apparently still going strong today. The Eccentrics found a highly appreciative audience amongst the Italian teenagers who were big fans of British pop music. Lead singer Mick Liddell got off with the most gorgeous girl in the Piper Club on practically the first night that the band played there. She was called Celli and he moved in with her almost immediately, afterwards he hardly ever went back to the hotel. The band had quite a wild stage act, sometimes Mick would play one of the cymbals on John's drum kit by repeatedly crashing a tambourine down on it which went down really well with the audience. One evening the unorthodox percussion technique resulted in breaking John's expensive Zildjian cymbal around the flange below the bell top. All attempts to repair it failed because the heat from the welding torch caused the thin beaten metal to distort and crack. These days a vintage "K" Zildjian cymbal made in Istanbul would be worth a considerable sum of money.

We weren't the first band from England to play at the club because "Colin Hicks & The Cabin Boys" were there before us and they had become very popular in Italy. Colin was the younger brother of pop star Tommy Steele and he had hired a British group called "The Shel Carson Combo" as his backing band. When The Cabin Boys split up the backing band called themselves "Il Rokes" and continued to tour Italy; they subsequently became extremely successful in their own right. (John Kerrison)

The other band playing at the Piper club called "Equipe Ottanta Quattro" (Team 84) were one of the biggest bands in Italy at that time. They had achieved considerable success in the Italian pop charts by recording American and British chart topping songs, substituting their own Italian lyrics. The band's hits included "Papa e Mamma" (a cover of "Papa Oom Mow Mow" by The Rivingtons) and "Ora puoi tornare" (a cover of "Go Now" by the Moody Blues). One day the Italian band members somehow discovered that it was Mick Liddell's nineteenth birthday and they invited The Eccentrics back to their hotel where they threw a party for him. There was "Prosecco" Italian white sparkling wine and cake, it was a nice gesture from the Italian band for the young British musicians who were such a long way from home in both distance and culture.

I went to the famous Fontana di Trevi with Peter Maggs... it's where the tourists chuck coins into the water. We had a beer in a nearby bar and listened to a song by Il Rokes on the juke box, but we weren't very impressed by it. I bought a really stylish pair of black brogues in a shoe shop across the road... West London Mods loved Italian shoes. (John Kerrison)

One night The Eccentrics were playing in the Piper club when a beautiful woman made a dramatic entrance surrounded by a protective male entourage, she was very glamorous and dressed in typically sophisticated Italian style. Everyone in the club was distracted by this stunning lady, including John; she noticed him staring at her and smiled back at him. The next evening John found a single red rose on the drum stool and he learned that the flower had been placed there by his newly acquired female admirer. It was a completely new experience for a working class teenager, things like that didn't usually happen in Hayes.

When a member of Equipe 84 had a birthday it provided an opportunity for The Eccentric's to return their hospitality and hold a party in their hotel. Franco Ceccarelli, the rhythm guitarist for the Italian band, could speak a little English. He took John to one side and advised him to steer clear of the woman who had made such an impression in the Piper club, he described her as the "Christine Keeler" of Rome. John of course failed to heed the caution given to him. When the lady in question returned to the club and asked him to sit with her during his break he readily agreed. In the Piper club there were areas on different levels and steps from the stage down to the dance floor so people could get quite close to the band if they wanted to. On either side of the performance area there was a staircase, each of which created a secluded alcove. Between his stints performing in the band John sat with the Italian woman in the left hand recess, he was rather intimidated by his mature glamorous companion.

The following evening she insisted that John should go back to her place and stay the night, he accepted her offer even though he was completely frightened and taken aback by such a forthright proposal. After the gig finished, at about 2.00 am, he left the Piper club and found a Fiat Seicento waiting outside; it was a model of car often used as a taxi in Italy. At the wheel there was a chauffeur

73

wearing a uniform complete with a peaked cap and John got into the back with the lady who immediately pounced on him. At only seventeen years of age he was totally out of his depth and, in a complete panic, he asked the driver to drop him off at the hotel. He never saw the woman again. John has only a few regrets about his teenage years and his adolescent lack of confidence that night is one of them. Later on John found romance with someone his own age whilst he performed in the Piper club. She was a seventeen year old Italian girl called Anna Maria Claudini and, as was the local custom, the couple were usually accompanied by a chaperone when they were together... but not always.

Chapter Ten

Musicians can be quite mercenary sometimes and a few are in it just for the money all of the time... but I was never a bread head. The money was important to me but it was never as important as the playing... right from the start, all that I ever wanted to do was to play the drums. (John Kerrison)

The Italian 1960s post war prosperity was evident everywhere in Rome and especially amongst the teenagers, their clothes had the style worshipped by British Mods. Beautiful elegant women were everywhere, they travelled nonchalantly perched riding side-saddle as passengers on the swarms of scooters which buzzed around the narrow streets, just like in the romantic films starring Sophia Loren or Audrey Hepburn shown in British cinemas. John loved the food, the architecture, the history and the people. He also developed a fascination for the Italian language and he started to learn a few words and phrases.

However, reminders of the misery endured during the wartime hostilities were still very apparent. John got to know the club bouncers and practised his new found linguistic skills by chatting with them. One evening, during a break between performances, he was talking to a doorman outside the Piper club. The bouncer, who was about forty years old, rolled up his shirt sleeve to show a number tattooed on his forearm like that seen on Holocaust survivors. The well built tough looking man said the Italian word *"Tedeschi"* meaning "Germans" whilst pulling a face in disgust. John surmised that the man had suffered the trauma of being incarcerated in a Nazi "death camp" during the war.

Just as The Eccentrics were about to finish their contract performing in Rome they got the chance to audition to play for a further month at a club, also called *Il Piper*, at the coastal town of

"Viareggio" in Northern Italy. They jumped at the chance to prolong their stay and decided to look their best by wearing their smart tailor-made blue mohair suits. This was the first time that the band had actually worn the clothes that their management had bought for them, instead of their usual attire of jeans and T-shirts, despite having given an interview back in England announcing that the scruffy look had gone out of fashion. The tactic of dressing up for the audition backfired when the owner of the club in Viareggio turned them down for the booking because he didn't like their clean cut well behaved image. Unfortunately he was looking for a rebellious British band who wore scruffy denim jeans and behaved badly.

The incident provoked an argument between John and his fellow band members and, in a combination of disappointment and homesickness, he announced that he was going home. The band tried to persuade him that if he stayed in Italy there was an opportunity to follow the success of bands like Equipe 84 and that they could all become millionaire pop stars, but John had made up his mind to leave. He borrowed fifteen pounds from the hotel manager, a sum of money which he regrets never having repaid, and set off for England. The long journey across Italy and France involved changing trains several times and John had to make sure that the traps cases containing his drum kit didn't get lost on the way. When he eventually reached London he telephoned his father who agreed to drive over to Victoria Railway Station and pick him up.

My dad asked me if I was glad to be home and I said that in one way I was but in another way I regretted leaving Italy. I told him that I wasn't sure what I was going to do next and he said, in his usual laid back way, that I should just sit back and see what happened next... I knew that I could always rely on my dad. (John Kerrison)

Mike Liddell stayed in Italy and teamed up with a band to form "Mike Liddell & Gli Atomi". When the remaining members of The Eccentrics, Peter Maggs and Roy Robinson, returned home they asked John to come to a meeting with their management at the offices of Ashley Sinclair. They attempted to convince him that he should go back to Italy with them, promising wealth and stardom, but he refused. Shortly afterwards Pete and Roy returned to Italy and teamed up with the bass guitarist and vocalist Romano Morandi from Equipe 84; he was deputising for Victor Sogliani who had been called up for National Service. Subsequently the band changed their name to "Romano and the Eccentrics" before going on tour. Their drummer was John "Speedy" Keen who later, as a member of the band "Thunderclap Newman", wrote a smash hit called "Something in the air".

The Bad Boys band from Northolt took over the residency at the *Il Piper* club in Rome and, somewhat coincidentally, John took a job working at the "Hallmarks" card factory in Northolt when he returned from Italy. Short of funds he sold his scooter and he had to catch the bus to get to work. However, the word that he was back home quickly got around the West London music scene and he soon started gigging again with any band that needed a drummer. Always at the back of John's mind was the thought that he should have returned to Rome with The Eccentrics. He also felt that in some ways he had let Peter down, especially as they had become quite close friends while sharing a hotel room in Italy; the pair did not speak to each other again for nearly fifty years. In all that time John believed that Peter held some animosity towards him but, when they got together recently, he found that it was not the case at all.

John turned eighteen on 4 August 1965 and, although now able to legally purchase alcohol, he was still regarded as a minor who was not old enough to vote. The age of majority, defining childhood from adulthood, was not lowered from the "key of the door" twenty-one down to eighteen until 1969. This change came about following a campaign which was instigated by John's friend Screaming Lord Sutch (the self appointed Earl of Harrow). Sutch formed "The National Teenage Party" which was a forerunner of the Official Monster Raving Loony Party.

Around October 1965 bass guitarist "Chip" Hawkes (later of "The Tremeloes") and vocalist Rodney Evans (who became the first lead singer for "Deep Purple") visited John and spent half a day trying to persuade him to join their band called "The Horizons". Together with lead guitarist Colin Butt the group had lined up a gig in Berlin but they didn't have a drummer. They hadn't heard John play the drums before and probably chose him without an audition solely because of his reputation, that and the small fact that at that time he was probably the only available drummer in West London who had a passport. Eventually John gave in and agreed to join them. Subsequently they all visited the East German Embassy and applied for visas which were stamped in their passports, a necessary requirement in order to cross the Warsaw Pact territory on the way to Berlin.

They set off on their long journey, all four of the band plus their gear crammed into a Bedford Dormobile, without rehearsing any of the songs that they intended to play. As they travelled through East Germany John was intrigued by the sight of a number of old women who were labouring in the cold and wet weather repairing the roads, he later realised that reason behind this female dominated workforce was the shortage of men left by the war. On the way to Berlin they stopped for one evening at a venue in Brunswick, where The Horizons had played the previous year, and they ran into another band from England called "The Quiet Five" who performing there. They generously allowed The Horizons to use their converted ambulance and get a good night's sleep before moving on the next morning. It was something of a luxury compared to the cramped conditions in the Bedford van which was packed full of gear.

There were a lot of British bands playing gigs all over Europe... it took a while for German bands to catch up with the demand for British style Rock & Roll in their own country. The Germans had really caught on to the Mod fashions but the Italians already had the style. (John Kerrison)

During their journey Chip decided to educate John by taking him on a sightseeing trip to the infamous Reeperbahn district in Brunswick. As they walked past the rows of windows where the prostitutes posed to advertise their wares Chip asked a particularly plump mature lady how much she charged. She told him that her fee was forty marks which, at an exchange rate of around eleven marks to one pound sterling, represented a considerably large sum of money in those days. Chip was older than John and much more brazen, he jokingly offered the woman forty pfennigs; a considerably trivial sum by any standard. "Forty pfennigs my arse," replied the portly prostitute in a broad Liverpudlian accent which took both young men by surprise. The pair of musicians continued to "window shop" further down the road and encountered a lady who was posing to attract customers until she suddenly recognised Chip, she ran away and hid out of sight behind the curtains. It turned out that Chip had dated the girl on his visit to Germany the previous year and he had been completely unaware of her occupation.

The club where The Horizons were booked to play was in the south-east borough of Berlin City called Neukölln. At night the band was contracted to play for three quarters of an hour each hour until all of the customers had left. One evening at around 02.30 am there were four male customers still drinking and listening to the band despite the late hour. Midway through a song John suddenly put down his drumsticks and stood up, he walked over to the men and shouted "Why don't you lot **** off?" at them. Despite the language barrier the German customers appeared to understand and promptly left, allowing the band to get some sleep; John may have been a skinny teenager but he had quite an attitude. On other occasions the band would repeatedly play nonsense songs like "A bicycle built for two" late at night in order to empty the club when they wanted to go to bed. However, the late hours were not the main problem. A much more pressing issue was money, the band did not get paid for the whole month that they performed at the club.

With little cash the band used to go to a local shop, which was only twenty to thirty yards down the road, and buy cheap items such as bread rolls and jam; they would also shoplift a Mars bar every time they went. They supplemented their meagre diet by stealing bratwurst sausages and drinks from behind the bar in the club. The only two decent meals that John can remember having during that month was pea soup once and, on another occasion, chicken and chips. He can still recall how delicious the food tasted in comparison to their usual mundane diet. Living under such basic conditions made it difficult to maintain any semblance of personal hygiene. The only place where they could get a proper wash or a shower was on a weekly visit to the central swimming baths, the pool was used as a location in the Bond movie "Octopussy" which was filmed in 1983.

We went to see the management at another club that they ran in central Berlin but they just kept making excuses about the money concerning contracts, work permits and whatever... the upshot was that they wouldn't pay us ... they had minders who looked like they had guns underneath their jackets... they were like real heavy gangsters. (John Kerrison)

The band had nothing to do all day while waiting for the club to open. They used to play on a table football machine for hours at a time, saving money by blocking both of the goals with pieces of cardboard to avoid having to insert any coins. John recalls that even while experiencing such penury he and the other smokers in the band could always somehow find enough money to buy cigarettes. However, when they still had not been paid after a whole month they all decided that it was time to quit. Colin Butt had to sell his Gibson 335 Stereo guitar in order to get petrol money for the homeward journey back to England, a loss which he never recouped. On the way they stayed in Hanover near another venue where The Horizons had played on a previous tour. They encountered a British band called "The Checkmates" who allowed them to bed down in their digs at the rear of the theatre.

When John arrived back in London he looked even skinnier than when he set off but his luck improved and he got a job with a firm called Aintry Structures who were based in Hanwell. It was there that he met Jack Rawlings who took John under his wing and taught him a great deal about carpentry. John was keen to learn from his mentor and these days he regards Jack, who is still working as a joiner at the age of eighty-three years old, as being part of his family. Around November 1965 he joined a band from Hounslow called "The Dae-B-Four". The group consisted of Ian Pitwell on lead vocals, Rex Brayley on lead guitar (he later played with "The Love Affair"), Brian Brayley on rhythm guitar and Roger Sidy played bass guitar. The Dae-B-Four was the epitome of a Mod pop band, somewhere between the "Small Faces" and the "The Who" in musical style and presentation. The Mod anthem "My Generation" figured heavily in their repertoire.

I used to get a lot of phone calls from musicians looking for a drummer because I was very well-known. I must have had a lot of status... Marshall's music shop was the hub for all of it. (John Kerrison)

The White Hart in Southall was a very important venue for Mod bands in the 1960s. The Who often played there and John performed there on many occasions with Frankie Read and the Casuals and then with The Eccentrics. The final time that John played at the White Hart was with The Dae-B-Four, it was a memorable event because he twisted his right ankle half way through the gig. Although it was a minor accident, just a slight sprain, the injury meant that John could not use his right foot to operate the bass drum pedal. All of his training and practice had involved using his left foot on the pedal for the hi-hat cymbals and the right foot on the bass drum pedal. He could not swop over and play the bass with his other foot, in the same way that it is near impossible for someone to change hands when writing. It soon became quite obvious that John would not be able to continue playing that evening and he went home. Rex Brayley could drum a bit so he put down his guitar and took over behind the drum kit for the rest of the gig. John soon recovered but the incident highlighted the extreme importance of the foot operated bass drum pedal for a Rock & Roll drummer, something that would later have much greater significance in John's drumming career.

Another band regularly on the bill at the White Hart was called "James Royal & the Hawks". When John played with Frankie Read and the Casuals they often crossed paths with The Hawks because they played the same venues, a great deal of good natured rivalry developed between the two bands. The Hawks appeared on the ITV television show "Ready, Steady, Go", taking part in a competition ingeniously titled "Ready, Steady, Win". They came second to "The Downliners Sect", a result which John and The Casuals felt was suspiciously unfair despite the Royals being their musical adversaries. Subsequently The Hawks changed their name to the "James Royal Set" and John played drums for them several times when they performed for the BBC Radio Light Programme. The musicians who accompanied vocalist Jimmy Royal in the sessions at the Maida Vale studios were drawn from an ad hoc pool and they played the sets with little or no rehearsal time together. John himself had a particularly relaxed and fairly blasé approach to drumming in the impromptu performances.

*We all knew the numbers and so we just got on with it, I guess...
All that you had to do when you were playing each song was to make
sure that everyone got in and got out (started and stopped) at the
same time... Jimmy Royal was a very nice guy and a very good
singer.*(John Kerrison)

Those who joined the fluid and ever changing line-up with the band playing on the radio show included keyboard player Rick Wakeman (later played with "Yes"), bass guitarist Nick Simper (later played with "Deep Purple"), bass guitarist Johnny Savage, guitarist Micky Borer, drummer Mick Underwood and several others from the world of Rock fame. They mainly played covers of well known Soul, Blues and Rock & Roll numbers. The Maida Vale studio was not exactly a beacon of new technology, the BBC didn't really do "keeping up-to-date" in those days. Everything changed around 1967 to 1968 when their sound studios went over to four or even eight track recording as they kept up with the fast pace of developments in the field of electronics. That it was very much an experimental phase was emphasised by the sound engineers who often wore white laboratory coats.

Broadcasting a "live" recording was something of a new concept at that time. The use of the term "live" was justified by the fact that the band were recorded playing together instead of on individual tracks. Working for the BBC all of the musicians should have all been paid at least the minimum rate for session players at that time, a situation enforced by the Musicians' Union. Such payments for the BBC sets was handled by Jimmy Royal's agent Mervyn Conn, a well known character in the music business. "Connie" was a cousin of comedian Bernie Winters and he managed a lot of big music shows and tours. Unfortunately John never received any money for playing with the James Royal Set.

Chapter Eleven

I watched the 1966 World Cup final on TV with all of my mates around our house. Although he was never much of a football fan my dad opened a bottle of champagne, God knows where he got it from. We all went up the West End in my mate's motor, it was a Standard Ten. There was quite a celebration going on, everyone was going mad and the atmosphere was fantastic. (John Kerrison)

In the summer of 1966 everyone was obsessed with the World Cup competition which was being hosted in England, with the final played at Wembley Stadium. One day John and his friends were hanging out in the Wimpy Bar at Ealing Broadway, a popular haunt for the scooter riding Mods, when a group of boisterous Italians football fans walked in. They were chanting for their national team and also directed some derogatory comments towards John and his companions in their native tongue, safe in the reasonable belief that what they were saying would not be understood. They were very surprised when John responded with some choice expletives in Italian which he had learned whilst he was staying in Rome. A bigger shock awaited them because Italy were eventually knocked out of the competition after a defeat in the group stages by a team from North Korea.

Shortly after England's historic World Cup victory, some of John's friends got hold of four tickets to fly to Nice. It was the first time that John had flown in an aeroplane, he and his friend Peter Veryard travelled together to join their pair of friends who had departed on an earlier flight. They decided to sleep on the beach in order to save money but the gendarmes had other ideas and woke them up at two in the morning to check their passports. The situation was far from satisfactory so John suggested to Peter that they should catch the train to Italy and look up Mike Liddell, the former front man for The Eccentrics had made his home there. When they arrived in Rome they telephoned Mike, but he was out, and his wife picked them up from the station. She drove John and Peter to the rehearsal rooms where Mike and his band "Gli Atomi" were practising.

After sleeping on the beach we went to the railway station in Nice. My mates went off and left me to look after the luggage... I bought a bottle of cheap red wine and drank it. I fell asleep on top of the bags and when I woke up there were red ants crawling all over me. (John Kerrison)

Mike asked John to join the band but told him that he could not sleep at his flat because his mother-in-law was staying and there was not enough room for anyone else. However, he knew someone who had a lock up shop with a bed in the basement. John agreed to join Gli Atomi and Peter went home back to London where he arranged for John's drum kit to be sent to Rome. Mike's band had quite a large following in Italy and, just like Equipe 84, they covered popular American and British hit songs which they extensively rewrote for the Italian music market. Mike Liddell & Gli Atomi got to the number three spot in the Italian pop charts with a number called "Nelle Mani Tue" which owed a great deal to "We can work it out" by the Beatles. The group's highly successful single "La Tua Immagine" was based upon "The Sound of Silence" by Simon & Garfunkel and the band gave a similar makeover to several other songs including "You Really Got Me" by The Kinks.

Gli Atomi went to a recording studio where John drummed on a track called "La Mia Inghilterra" (My England), which was released on the ARC label (Catalogue No. AN 4098). In the evenings John would retire to the shop basement which was then locked from the outside, leaving him imprisoned until the next morning, it was a less than perfect situation. Eventually the claustrophobic overnight surroundings became intolerable and John decided to return home but he had insufficient funds to do so. Mike Liddell gave John a lift and dropped him off at the British Embassy in the Via 20 Settembre. The Embassy officials were very helpful, they booked him into a nearby hotel and the manager invited him to dinner at his house that evening.

84

The next day John had to wait whilst telephone calls were made to his parents in England, they would be required to act as guarantors for payment of his hotel bill and train ticket home. Whilst he waited in the Piazza del Popolo, which is situated just down the road from the Spanish Steps, he saw a street vendor selling some nice looking grapes. He bought a couple of huge bunches with the small amount of money that he had. Eating such a large quantity of fruit after an existence level diet had a sudden and violently volcanic laxative effect on his gastric system. Despite an Olympic sprint he failed to reach the hotel in time and it was fortunate that he had a spare pair of clean Y-fronts in his luggage. In a rather ignoble gesture he discarded his soiled underwear out through the hotel toilet window.

Whilst John was crossing Europe by train bound for England his drum kit was travelling in the opposite direction to Italy. It was a pleasant surprise when he was reunited with his drum kit which followed him home a short while later and arrived at his parents' house in Hayes with absolutely nothing broken or missing. He also had the good fortune to regain his job working in the joiner's shop and he soon began gigging in the evenings again.

I was like a scarecrow when I was young and I used to smoke forty fags a day. If you see pictures of me when I was nineteen, I was like a skeleton. It's only through being in the (wheel) chair that my shoulders have got really built up. (John Kerrison)

One day in October 1966 John was in London and he was shocked when he read the newspaper headlines reporting the tragic death of Johnny Kidd. The Rock & Roll legend had been killed whilst travelling in the front passenger seat of a Jaguar which had been involved in a collision with another vehicle. John had seen Johnny Kidd and the Pirates perform at the Southall Community Centre at the height of their popularity in the early 1960s. The band members all famously dressed in pirate costumes whilst Kidd himself wore an eye patch as his "signature" gimmick plus he sported a cutlass hanging from his belt; he repeatedly performed cowboy booted high leg kicks along to the music. The band and their skull and crossed bones pirate flag were illuminated on stage by a "UV" ultra violet light source. The rather eerie blue glow increased the awe factor amongst their audience because many ordinary people had never seen the strange fluorescent phenomenon before.

The Pirates pretty much invented the line-up of having a non playing lead singer fronting the group plus a single "lead" guitarist and a bass player with the drummer at the rear; a highly successful format which was adopted by most of the Rock bands that followed afterwards. "Kiddo" had been a huge star and, prior to his death, he was experiencing something of a renaissance touring as "Johnny Kidd and The New Pirates" with a fresh line-up comprising of Nick Simper on bass guitar, Mickey Stewart on lead guitar, Johnny Carroll on keyboards and Roger "Solly" Truth on drums. John had known Nick Simper from the days when they had both hung around in Jim Marshall's music shop; at that time John was about fifteen and Nick, two years older at seventeen, was a budding guitarist who only later switched to playing the bass.

The Pirates reckoned that Solly had short arms and long pockets when it came to paying his way. One evening he stayed in the van whilst the band went to get beef burgers... as usual he promised to pay for his burger when they got back, but nobody believed him. Nick Simper put some beer mats in a bread roll with a load of tomato sauce and gave it to Solly as a joke for being tight with his money. (John Kerrison)

A few months after the tragedy John got a call from Nick who had recently recovered from the injuries which he sustained in the same car crash which took Johnny Kidd's life. The Pirates were attempting to reform and were looking for a replacement drummer. Roger Truth had originally agreed to play for them but he left to drum for a Soul band which was headed by a former light heavyweight boxer from the USA called Freddie Mack. The sudden departure of the drummer left The Pirates in the lurch because they were already booked to go on tour. John subsequently passed an audition for the band and rehearsed with them a couple of times at the Southall Community Centre, which was coincidentally the same venue where he had first seen Johnny Kidd and the Pirates perform. Nick Simper was particularly impressed by John's ability to learn so many new numbers in such a short time.

The band was managed by a lady called Joan Watson who was the proprietress of the Organ Centre music shop in Ealing. She was in her mid fifties and, due to a medical condition, she had extraordinarily large eyes. Her music shop was well known amongst those who were involved in the West London music scene and she had many contacts in the music business. Joan was a great help to several up and coming young musicians in the 1960s. The Pirates without Johnny Kidd were an unknown commodity but their enterprising manager succeeded in getting them booked at venues in the West Country and in Scotland. A van was hired to carry the band and their gear which included "Leslie" speakers for the Hammond C3 organ. The speakers faced downwards and, due to an innovative rotating sound system, produced a characteristic resonance which was part of The Pirates' musical style.

The Hammond organ split into two parts when it had to be lifted about. The bottom half was relatively light but the top half weighed a ton. (John Kerrison)

In early 1967 The Pirates played at three venues in the West Country, starting with the Naval helicopter base at Helston followed by Penzance and then the Blue Lagoon dance hall in Newquay. In Penzance they spotted a bed and breakfast aptly named "The Pirates' Hotel" and instantly chose it as a place to stay for the evening. John stepped in a deposit left by the landlady's dog, much to the amusement of his fellow band members. However, worse was to come later when the canine music critic singled out John's bed to make a further excremental statement as to his opinion of the band. John was the only member of The Pirates who was unable to see the funny side of the incident.

There were some quite justifiable concerns that The Pirates, in the absence of Johnny Kidd, might receive a rather poor reception. Micky and Nick's vocals were pretty good but they were no substitute for the hugely charismatic Kiddo who was worshipped by his numerous female admirers. All of the band members were seasoned professionals and they performed Johnny Kidd's well known chart toppers, including "Shakin' all over" with its iconic drum break, very competently. Fortunately they were well received by an appreciative audience, there was even some screaming from the female fans and a lot of requests for autographs. The short tour of the West Country was quite successful and the band returned to London in high hopes of obtaining a recording contract in the near future.

In Glasgow they played for three days at the famous Kelvin Hall on the same bill as "Unit 4 plus 2" and "Dave Dee, Dozy, Beaky, Mick and Titch". Also present was Screaming Lord Sutch who, performing in a Roman centurion costume, had renamed his support band "The Holy Roman Empire". Ironically the Rock & Roll extravaganza also featured the Freddie Mack Band and defecting drummer Roger Truth came in for a considerable amount of good natured ribbing from his former associates in The Pirates. The gig was spread over the weekend and The Pirates opened each of the twice daily performances. One evening Lord Sutch handed Nick Simper a sabre and challenged him to a pretend sword fight on stage during his usual outrageous performance. Nick fled when he came close to having an arm lopped off by the seriously deranged Rocker. Most of the bands stayed in the same hotel which was situated in Glasgow's Sauchiehall Street and it was there that John got his first introduction to smoking cannabis.

One day John found a member of The Pirates who was on his hands and knees sniffing at the base of the locked hotel bedroom door where members of Dave Dee, Dozy, Beaky, Mick, and Titch were ensconced. He was apparently attempting to detect if they were smoking dope in their room. Later John smoked cannabis for the first time himself and, completely stoned, began performing acrobatics by jumping off the wardrobe onto the bed. He recalls that it was probably Nick Simper who dared him to run down three flights of stairs and drop his pyjama trousers, flashing at the shocked pedestrians passing by the hotel in Sauchiehall Street. Rock musicians often make their own fun when they're resting between gigs.

At that time I didn't really see any casualties from drug taking amongst the musicians that I knew... after the accident I saw some people get damaged, mainly by cocaine. If you smoke dope and play the drums everything seems to slow down... you start thinking to yourself "this isn't half slow tonight". (John Kerrison)

Not everyone in Glasgow was a fan of The Pirates. After the final gig the band parked their hire van to get something to eat before heading back to their hotel. John Kerrison and Johnny Carroll waited in the vehicle whilst Nick Simper and Mickey Stewart went to buy some food from a stall. When a group of men who were standing nearby heard a request for four teas and four pies spoken in a distinct London accent they responded by shouting "Sassenachs". The two Pirates ran and hid in the van but the hire company address, Hanwell London W7, painted on the rear doors was a bit of a giveaway as to their English ethnicity. A well aimed missile shattered one of the vehicle's back windows as the band made a quick getaway with Nick behind the wheel. There was a lot of explaining to do, not to mention a hefty surcharge, when they returned the van to the hire company.

Back in London the band regrouped in Joan Watson's music shop where they leaned that she had been unable to get them a recording contract or obtain bookings for any further gigs. There appeared to be little future in continuing to fly the Jolly Roger flag and The Pirates made a mutually agreed decision to break up and go their separate ways. John retuned to his parents' house and went back to his job working in the joiner's shop. There were still plenty of local bands who needed a drummer, especially one who had played with The Pirates. All that John had to do was wait for the telephone to ring.

Ian Gillan was one of those who were seeking to employ John's talent as a drummer. The future Deep Purple frontman had just returned from a very successful three month stint in Beirut as the lead vocalist with a band called "Episode Six". He invited John and bass guitarist Steve Priest to a meeting, at the Queen's Head public house in Cranford, where he put forward a proposal that they set up a band to play in Beirut. The plan being to cash in on the potential demand for British style Rock & Roll created in the wake of Episode Six's sell-out performances in the Lebanese capital. John and Steve were to recruit a band whilst Ian would act as their agent, booking the gigs and making all the necessary arrangements. Ian suggested that they enlist lead guitarist Tony Tacon, who had been with him in The Javelins, but in the end the project failed to get off the ground.

Later that summer in 1967 John's friend and namesake called John, who was known as "Harry-Harry", asked him to go on holiday to Greece. John did not have the required twenty-one pounds to pay for the vacation but Harry-Harry agreed to lend him the money which was to be repaid afterwards at a pound a week. Harry-Harry was also a drummer but not a professional, he worked in his father's grocery shop in Hayes. The pair flew from London to Rimini and then on to Ancona by coach. There was a day and a half sea cruise down to Petras followed by a coach ride to the camp site at Xylokastro. An optional three day sea cruise went around the islands taking in sights such as Santorini, Mykonos, Hydra and Delos. John recalls that he and Harry-Harry also went on a precarious donkey ride up to the summit of the ancient volcanic crater on the island of Santorini.

The two lads from Hayes really enjoyed themselves. Harry-Harry did more than sunbathe and soak up the local history, he lost his virginity. Holiday romance was also in the air for John when he met a Lancashire lass from Salford called Linda, she arrived in Greece about five days after him and as soon as he saw her he was smitten. She was no doubt equally taken by the six foot tall slim Londoner who dressed in fashionably smart Mod gear and played the drums in Rock bands. They spent their time together listening to the local band playing traditional Greek music, eating at the open air restaurant and sitting on the beach drinking orange juice mixed with Ouzo. John recalls that the song "A Whiter Shade of Pale" by the British Rock band "Procol Harum" was in the UK pop charts that summer and it was being played everywhere. When it was time for John and Linda to return home they exchanged addresses and kept in touch by letter and on the telephone, a complete breach of the rules concerning such holiday romances.

Salford is a long way from Hayes and John was soon dating a local girl called Annie Fairweather who he had met at a party. He had sold his scooter shortly after returning home from Italy and so, without any transport of his own, he often borrowed his mother's moped to go to meet his new girlfriend. Annie's father was a GPO telephone engineer, he and John always got on well together.

However, John always addressed him as "Mr Fairweather" and never referred to him by his first name; such well mannered formality was very much the norm at that time. Mr Fairweather was quite laid back and he had no qualms about his daughter dating a Rock & Roll drummer. Nevertheless, he strongly advised John to learn a trade, something which he could fall back on just in case his ambition to be a professional musician faltered. They were wise words which all young men embarking on a career in Rock & Roll music should heed.

Chapter Twelve

When I did the audition for Episode Six it was between me and another guy, I can't remember who… I was nineteen and the other guy was younger than me. Afterwards Roger Glover said to me "I liked the way that you played John, there was something about your eyes". (John Kerrison)

A short while after John retuned from Greece Ian Gillan got in contact again and this time he offered John the chance to audition for Episode Six. John jumped at the chance, the band were hot news in all of the music papers and they had just completed a very successful three month tour in Beirut at the "Casino du Liban". The Episode Six line-up comprised Ian Gillan as lead vocalist, Harvey Shield on drums, Tony Barham on lead guitar, Sheila Dimmock on vocals and keyboards, her brother Graham Carter Dimmock on rhythm guitar and Roger Glover on bass guitar. A vacancy for a drummer had opened in the band when Harvey Shield had given notice that that he wanted to resign. John was invited to watch Episode Six perform and he took his girlfriend Annie to see the band when they played in Slough.

Harvey Shield's drumming style was different to mine, he was a bit softer… he also added his vocals to the band, whereas I can't sing at all. Harvey wrote a song called "The Way I Feel Tonight" which was a hit for the "Bay City Rollers". (John Kerrison)

John passed the audition to join Episode Six and, thinking that this could be the big chance that he had been waiting for, he bought a new drum kit from Jim Marshall's music shop. It was a Premier kit in an oyster blue finish consisting of a pair of 22" x 14" bass drums plus 12" x 8", 14" x 8" and 16" x 16" tom-toms; all with high quality

Roger Sivomatic fittings and pedals. A Jazz drummer called Louie Bellson had pioneered playing twin bass drums and their use was adopted later by Rock & Roll drummers such as Ginger Baker, Ainsley Dunbar and Cozy Powell to produce what would later be known as the "Heavy" or "Hard" genre of Rock music. However, John found the double bass drum format difficult to master and transporting the extra equipment to gigs was also a problem.

Bass drumming technique was in its infancy in the sixties... we would play with the whole of the right foot on the pedal. In the seventies and eighties they developed a technique called "kicking the bass drum"... it meant hitting the bass drum pedal with just the toe, the heel was raised off the floor. Then it progressed to hitting the pedal with the toe and heel together, all in one movement, to get two beats. A friend of mine called Steve Holland can do it real quick using both feet on twin bass drums. (John Kerrison)

Although John specifically purchased the two bass drums to play with Episode Six he only used the twin bass drum set up at one gig with the band. The venue was the Clay Pigeon public house at Eastcote which he chose to trial playing the two bass drums because it was near his home. Even then he had to take one of the large bass drums in his car because there was not enough room for it along with the rest of his kit and the band's gear in the van. A drummer called Mick Tucker came to watch the band play, he met John in the Gents toilets and complimented him by saying that his drumming was very precise. A few years later Mick began using the two bass drum format in his own kit when he played with the 1970s Glam Rock band "The Sweet"; coincidentally the group's bass guitarist and backing vocalist Steve Priest was in the year below John at Mellow Lane Comprehensive School in Hayes.

Mitch Mitchell had twin bass drums but he was a bit too flowery for my liking. In my view he played far too much for himself and not for the song... When he was young he got a lot of work with different bands but they often ended up sacking him because he overplayed. Sometimes he did far too many drum-fills ... less is more. (John Kerrison)

Episode Six were managed by a lady called Gloria Bristow who, for one reason or another, was known as "Glorious Bristols". She had worked for Helmut Gordon when he was manager for The Who. Flower Power was now the fashion and the band were taken down to Carnaby Street to choose clothes as part of their "Peace and Love" stage image. John was very reluctant to give up his Mod style but he had to conform and wear the hippy gear that the management had bought for him. His smart tailored suits were replaced by velvet flared trousers, beads, bells and a kaftan tunic. John's sister made him a green velvet shirt with huge lapels. He also had a couple of Lee denim jackets which his girlfriend Annie dyed for him, one was bright orange and the other was a rather lurid lime green. Gigs had been lined up for Episode Six to play at major venues in the UK and further afield in Europe, which necessitated all of the band members joining the MU (Musicians' Union). They also joined Equity, becoming members of the actors' union in case they got involved in any film work.

I think that the MU is a very good thing, especially around the session stuff, so that everybody gets paid at least the set rate. The rest of the time it's all a question of if you give us a hundred quid we do the gig, if you are only offering fifty notes then we aren't turning up. (John Kerrison)

Most of the band's sound system was obtained from the "Sound City" shop in Shaftesbury Avenue which was run by someone called Ivan Arbiter. He was a big importer of musical equipment and he ran another establishment in London's West End called "Drum City". Episode Six had an impressive amount of "on-stage" equipment which included six Sound City 4 x 12 cabinet speakers, John's extensive drum kit, the bass guitar amplifier rig, the electronic organ plus all the auxiliary gear such as microphone stands and cables. The band needed somewhere to practise and John suggested booking the rehearsal rooms at Southall Community Centre.

John had been going out with Annie for more than a year after they had met. He was also still in contact with his girlfriend Linda in Salford. His infatuation with the Northern girl, which began on holiday in Greece, had not diminished despite their geographical separation. When Annie returned back home to Hayes from a trip to Ostend John decided to come clean about his affair and he took her for a walk along the Grand Union Canal. They sat down at a place known locally as the Pack Hills and had a long talk. He told her about his relationship with Linda and they parted company on fairly amicable terms. However, John still regrets not having ever properly apologised to Annie and he believes that he let her down badly.

After only a week of rehearsal sessions it was time for the band to set off for Germany in a van, it gave John very little time to learn so many songs. Their first booking was at the Storyville Club in Cologne where, after the first gig, John dragged Tony Barham to a disco across the road. It was a culture shock for the lead guitarist who was far more used to going back to the hotel with the rest of the band after performing. The club held a surprise for both John and Tony, it turned out to be a gay bar and its female clientele were far more interested in each other than the two British Rock musicians.

John had played in several different bands and deputised for the drummer in many other groups, as a result he was very adaptable when joining an established band. He changed the sound of Episode Six with his drumming technique by playing in a style that was "heavier" than his predecessor Harvey Shield and, in his own words, he gave it a bit more physical "wallop". The Episode Six repertoire consisted almost entirely of cover songs, putting their own slant on the hit numbers of the day. The songs that they played were very varied and diverse. Their sets included covers of numbers from "The Doors", "Love", "Aretha Franklin", "Sandie Shaw", "Gene Pitney", "Simon and Garfunkel", "The Rolling Stones", "The Grateful Dead" and "Harry Belafonte". The wide range of musical genres and styles encompassed by the band enabled John to demonstrate his versatility as a drummer.

When I played on stage with Episode Six I still didn't have the drums miked up despite having to compete with the increased sound wattage from the amps. It was the first time that I had the band's name on the front of my bass drum. In The Eccentrics I played without any front on the bass, it makes no difference to the sound.
(John Kerrison)

After Cologne Episode Six played at another Storyville club in Frankfurt for a further week; they performed on stage every night until around 11.00 pm. On evening after the gig John and some of the other band members went down the road to the city's red light district. In Kaiserstrasse they found a club called "K52" where British musician Alan Price was performing. The waiters carried huge trays full of beers balanced above their heads on the upturned palms of their hands. They served the customers, swerving around the tables, whilst theatrically threatening a disaster without actually spilling a drop of beer. Unfortunately one waiter passed close by the stage just as Alan Price stood up to acknowledge the applause from the audience and the drinks went flying. It was quite a spectacle.

The Kinks were very big at that time. The lead guitarist Dave Davies came to the Storyville club in Frankfurt and he got on stage with us, but he was very drunk and it was probably not his best performance. (John Kerrison)

After returning home to the UK the band immediately embarked on another demanding tour. Dave King was a drummer who John had met in the Ealing Jazz Club and he often used to give John a lift in his Ford Anglia whenever he went to an Episode Six gig. John recalls that Dave was "as mad as a March hare behind the wheel", which is quite some criticism from a man with a notoriously demented style of driving. The band played at several universities up and down the UK, often they were "all-nighters" with several acts performing one after the other right through the evening.

We must have looked really flash because we had top equipment and a brand new six-wheeled Ford Transit van. When we played at a gig in Northampton the bass guitarist from an "up north" band took offence. He was a right hard man... he walked up and took a leak on our "southern poncey" van. Ian Gillan was the only one of us who went and challenged him. (John Kerrison)

During that time Episode Six played on the same bill with top bands such as "Status Quo", "The Move" plus the psychedelic Rock group "Simon Dupree and the Big Sound". At Manchester University they performed alongside "Chris Farlowe and the Thunderbirds" and John's holiday romance girlfriend Linda came over from Salford to see him play, she was heavily pregnant. The pair had kept in touch and John was aware that she was expecting a baby by another man. He was still infatuated with her and he visited her whenever the band had a gig within travelling distance to Salford.

I was never really into all the sixties Flower Power psychedelic stuff like the rest of them were. Roger Glover was always reading a hippy underground magazine called "IT" (International Times) ... *but these days he says that he doesn't remember doing so.* (John Kerrison)

The band cut a track called "I can see through you" in the Pye recording studios near Marble Arch which was released on the PYE label (Catalogue No. 7N 17376). John quite liked the song which was written by bass guitarist Roger Glover. For some reason he did not drum on the B side of the record which was a cover of Nat King Cole's "When I fall in love". Unfortunately the single failed to make any impression in the pop charts when it was released, possibly because it was poorly promoted by Pye and it received little airtime on radio. John believes that the song deserved to have done better. Shortly afterwards Episode Six were on their way back to Germany again.

The Blow-Up Club in Munich was named after the 1966 film in which David Hemmings played the part of a trendy "Swinging Sixties" fashion photographer. It was a huge venue with a stage high up on a balcony where the bands played to the audience who were one floor below. Episode Six were booked to play there for sixteen nights and John discovered that the club was paying a performance fee amounting to sixteen hundred pounds. It was a quite staggering amount compared to the ten pounds a week that each band member was receiving. He expressed his dissatisfaction concerning the situation to Tony and told him that wanted to repay his mother the hundred pounds that he owed her. The guitarist said that he also owed his mother a hundred pounds and it ended up with the band rallying together to ask for more money. Subsequently each band member got a hundred pounds to "repay their mothers".

I don't remember ever really having stage fright in front of big audiences. You are kind of hidden behind the drum kit... I only worried about it if I went out from behind the drums. (John Kerrison)

Episode Six recorded a television film in Germany to promote their single, a very early example of a pop video. It was shot in the Olympic stadium in Hamburg where Hitler had famously snubbed the black American athlete Jesse Owens shortly before World War II. Sheila was frozen and they kept giving her brandy to warm her up, as a result of the repeated attempts to ward off the chill she became really quite drunk. John went out with a young lady in Munich who worked in a bar. Late at night after the gigs she used to take him back to her parents' apartment and then kicked him out at five o'clock in the morning before his presence was detected. "The Equals" played at the Blow-Up Club after Episode Six and the girl married one of the band members. Sometime later she turned up at the Kerrison's house in Hayes looking for John but he had gone away and he never found out why she had tried to see him.

Early in 1968 the band left PYE and Gloria Bristow negotiated a new deal with MGM; at the same time Episode Six shortened their name to "The Episode". They cut a track called "Little One" at the Lansdowne Recording Studio in Lansdowne Road Notting Hill which had a four track system. The song was written by Wadey and Grainger; they penned "Black is Black" which was a hit for "Los Bravos". Little One was produced by former "Springfields" guitarist Mike Hurst and released on the MGM label (Catalogue No. MGM-1409). The B side was called "Wide Smiles" and was written by Ian Gillan and Roger Glover, it was probably their first recorded collaboration before they teamed up together again in Deep Purple the following year.

In order to promote the band's single MGM held a photo shoot at an upmarket trendy restaurant nightclub called "Hatchetts". Situated in London's Piccadilly, diagonally opposite the Ritz Hotel, the clubs clientele included many of the famous bands of that era and several well known TV personalities also hung out there. Episode Six were photographed posing inside and outside Hatchetts holding cute cuddly lion cubs alongside an electric car made predominantly from glass. The lion cubs represented the famous MGM roaring lion mascot but the relevance of the glass car was somewhat more obscure. John recalls that Sheila attracted far more attention than the rest of the band and the lion cubs put together.

The photographers were much more interested in photographing Sheila who was wearing a short mini skirt, they were trying to get a shot of her knickers. (John Kerrison)

The band recorded a set for Southern ITV at their Southampton studios for a programme called *"Time for Blackburn"*. The show was compered by disc jockey Tony Blackburn and a group called "Unit Four plus Two" were there as well, they had a number one hit with a song called "Concrete and Clay". The Episode also recorded a huge number of tracks for the BBC which were played on the "Radio One Club". At the same time the band were touring around the UK. They played a cover of the Doors' "Light My Fire" which they extended to more than ten minutes and the performance included a stage fight in the middle with Ian and Graham rolling around on the floor. At some point scattering five big boxes of corn flakes all over the stage followed by a lot of crazy foam regularly became part of their riotous finale. The audience loved it but the mess that it left on stage did not make them at all popular with the venue's caretakers who had to clear up afterwards.

Dr TRIPLETT'S PRIMARY SCHOOL 1957. John Kerrison is kneeling in the front row with his hands on the ground. On his left is Steve Priest - the future bass guitarist in "The Sweet".

John Kerrison aged 11 years in the rear garden at 50 Botwell Common Road.

THE COSSACKS Hayes Park "Battle of the Bands" 1961.
Left to right Keith Lewis lead guitar/vocals, unknown rhythm guitarist,
John Kerrison, Mervyn Lewis bass guitar.
Note the Watkins Dominator amplifier at front.

PAUL & THE ALPINES Hayes Park "Battle of the Bands" 1962.
Left to right Ray Kirkham lead guitar, John Kerrison, Dave Dove bass
guitar, Dave Bone piano, Alf Fripp rhythm guitar.

John Kerrison performs a drum solo in Wistowe House 1962 watched by Ray Kirkham. John autographed the photo for the sister of the drummer in Ian Gillan's band The Javelins.

PAUL & THE ALPINES 1962. Left to right Ray Kirkham lead guitar, John Kerrison, Dave Dove bass guitar, Paul Lonergan vocals, and Alf Fripp rhythm guitar.

PAUL & THE ALPINES Wistowe House 1962.
Left to right Ray Kirkham lead guitar, John Kerrison, Alf Fripp rhythm
guitar and Dave Dove bass guitar.

THE CASUALS Ealing Town Hall early 1963.
Left to right Ian Holland lead guitar, John Kerrison, Frankie Reid lead
vocals and Steve Hargreaves bass guitar.

THE CASUALS Botwell House 1963.
Left to right Chris Jackson rhythm guitar, Reg Bodman bass guitar, John Kerrison, Frankie Reid lead vocals and Mick Liber lead guitar.

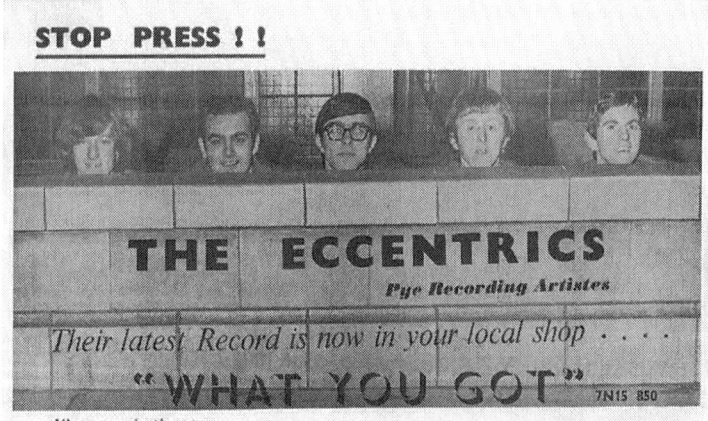

Handbill "flyer" to publicise the release of The Eccentrics' single "What You Got" 1964. Left to right Peter Maggs, Bruce Watts, Mick Liddell, Roy Robinson and John Kerrison.

John photographed behind his Premier drum kit and Ludwig snare, playing with Frankie Reid and the Casuals at Botwell House supporting The Rolling Stones.

The Eccentrics posing for a publicity shoot on the London Embankment wearing their smart new suits, demonstrating that the scruffy look was no longer fashionable.

EPISODE SIX - Left to right - Graham Carter Dimmock, John Kerrison, Ian Gillan, Sheila Dimmock, Tony Barham and Roger Glover. Photograph by Doug McKenzie.

John's younger sister Barbara   *John with his older sister Annette*

Clare and Ernest Kerrison - John's wonderful parents.

John Kerrison in a recent portrait - he still hates being photographed in his wheelchair.

Chapter Thirteen

Apparently Ian Gillan said about me later that I was "a character and a half"... I can't even begin to think what he meant by that.
(John Kerrison)

One evening after a gig the band encountered an Episode fan who turned out to be the daughter of a famous big band leader, a saxophonist and composer called Ken Mackintosh. In the 1950s and early 1960s he penned several tunes, some of which achieved chart success. Ken and his band were regularly featured on BBC Radio and they would often accompany famous singers such as Shirley Bassey or Tom Jones when they were on tour. He invited The Episode band members back to his house where John met his fifteen year old son who was known as "Andy Mack". The teenager was something of a musical prodigy and had been writing complex scores since the age of twelve.

Ken Mackintosh used to hire a hall in Streatham where his Swing band rehearsed on Sunday mornings. John accepted Ken's invitation to practise with the band and he regularly drove to the rehearsal sessions in his sister's battered old Ford Anglia. Despite his youthful arrogance he always listened to Ken's constructive criticism of his drumming.

I soon realised that, despite having gained an enormous amount of practical experience, my ability to play from sheet music was not up to scratch. (John Kerrison)

John found some of his fellow band members in The Episode to be a little precious and lightweight on occasion and, in comparison to his own self admitted outspoken "loudmouth" arrogance, they probably were. His tendency to speak his mind no matter what the circumstances often caused friction and John began to regularly fall out with Graham Carter Dimmock in particular. One day the rhythm guitarist was reading an Ian Fleming novel when John made a comment about the actor who played James Bond in the film. Graham corrected John's mispronunciation of "Sean" Connery with a great deal of sarcasm which added to the ill feeling already present. Such tensions often occur amongst the members of a band in the cheek by jowl proximity of touring and, with John's unforgiving forthright disposition, it was a complete certainty that things could only get worse.

The band had no roadies when they were on tour. Having the luxury of muscular men on hand to carry and set up the gear only came about later with bigger bands, larger venues and the advent of more complex equipment. The band members themselves had to load and unload all of their gear at the "get in" and the "get out" for every gig. It was quite hard work especially when there was a double gig at two different locations in the same evening and a particularly arduous task after having expended so much energy during a performance. Many a good musician from the 1960s now has back problems which were caused by having to carry the cumbersome weight of a Hammond C3 electric organ, plus all the other heavy sound equipment, back and forth from the van to the stage.

Drummers often used to set up their kit on a piece of carpet or they tied the seat to the spurs on the drums with a piece of string... it was done to stop the kit wondering away during a gig. I used to hammer nails into the stage in front of the bass drum... I did that all over the place including Italy and Germany. They didn't mind my "carpentry" in the venues... mainly because they didn't know about it. (John Kerrison)

Graham did not assist when the band's gear was being loaded and unloaded, claiming an exemption from the heavy work on account of his being the van driver. One evening whilst he was driving back from Manchester he announced that he was going to stop and have a short nap. John volunteered to take his place behind the wheel so that the band would not be delayed on their way home. However, Graham refused to let him drive, possibly having previous experience of

John's exciting driving style, and he parked up to take a rest. Nevertheless, the guitarist probably managed to get very little beneficial sleep because John deliberately disturbed his slumber by drumming random percussion riffs on the dashboard with his hands. Around July 1968 the situation came to a head when John set up his drum kit on the other side of the stage at a gig and played in glorious isolation from the rest of the band. The tactic did not go down well with either his fellow musicians or the band's manager Gloria Bristow.

I always got on well with Ian (Gillan), we had been friends since I was fifteen. On tour with The Episode we often shared a hotel bedroom and whenever we were gigging near my home he stayed at our house. When my dad was away working we slept in my parents' bed and my mum slept in my bed. Roger Glover was a nice guy, very laid back... he and Ian became close friends after they met in Episode Six. (John Kerrison)

Subsequently John was summoned to a meeting at Gloria Bristow's basement flat in Aylesford Street Pimlico where he was given the sack and paid twenty-five pounds as severance money. The rest of the band were also present and John's dismissal appeared to be a somewhat unanimous decision because no one spoke up in his defence. John's drum kit was still in the van and it was dropped of at his house shortly afterwards. Mick Underwood (who later joined "The Herd") was recruited to take John's place in the band. The choice of Mick Underwood as a replacement drummer may well have been influenced by his style of drumming which was very similar to that employed by John; an unsurprising coincidence in view of the fact that they were both former students of drum tutor and amplifier legend Jim Marshall.

I always liked Micky "Underpants", he was a very nice guy and a really good drummer... but I shouldn't have been sacked... I could stick it down a bit and Mick Underwood could stick it down a bit as well... I think that we both gave the band a heavier sound. (John Kerrison)

John sought the advice of his peers and mentors in Jim Marshall's music shop where he expressed his woes concerning getting sacked from the band. Chris Sherwood was now the shop manager, he had given John his first gig when he was only thirteen and he was very experienced in the music business. He agreed with John that the amount that he had been paid as severance money was a bit on the low side, but he advised him to forget any potentially costly breach of contract action and just get on with finding another band. In any event such changes in the line-up were a frequent occurrence and brought about the evolution of several bands which went on to achieve legend status.

The recordings of Episode Six "Cornflakes and Crazyfoam" (PUR 329D 1 & 2) and "The Radio 1 Club Sessions 68/69" (RPM 178) are an interesting insight into the nascent stages of Deep Purple. Further albums produced from the band's recorded live performances and studio sessions include "Put Yourself in My Place (released 1987), "The Complete Episode Six: The Roots of Deep Purple" (released 1991) and "Love Hate Revenge: File Under Deep Purple" (released 2005).

When John turned twenty-one on 4 August 1968 he held a birthday party in the front room of his parents' house in Botwell Common Road. Linda came down from Lancashire to join in with the celebrations and, despite their long term relationship, she slept in a separate bedroom from John. She had by now given birth and her baby boy was being looked after by her mother back in Salford. Many of John's family and friends, including Nick Simper, came to the party. Earlier that year Nick had become a founding member of a new band called Deep Purple and he brought with him a copy of the Heavy Rock group's recently released first album titled "Shades of Deep Purple".

The psychedelic Rock album had been recorded at the Pye Studios in Marble Arch where John had previously recorded a single with Episode Six. The guests at John's party were given the privilege of hearing one of the first public airings of the album. Derek Radburn, one of John's old friends that he had grown up with, pronounced that the album was "a load of crap". Nick responded to the caustic appraisal by snatching the record off the turntable and storming out. Shades of Deep Purple did not sell at all well in the UK

111

but it is nevertheless regarded by many people these days as being a ground breaking achievement. The album gained much greater recognition in the USA where the track "Hush", written by Joe South, was a hit single. Another track called "Love help me" is notable due to Nick Simper's outstanding rendition of the song's prominent bass line.

There were usually several drummers hanging around Ken Mackintosh's rehearsal studio in Streatham and one of them, on hearing that John had been sacked from The Episode, said that he would put him up for an audition with a band called "Don Lang & his Frantic Five". In the 1950s the group had released several singles and they were the resident band on the BBC pop music programme "*The Six-Five Special*", plus they also recorded the programme's theme tune. Yorkshireman Don Lang later played trombone on a Beatles' track called "Revolution 1" which, released on their famous 1968 "White Album", was a blues version of their hit single "Revolution".

John played at an audition for the Frantic Five at the Empire Ballroom in Leicester Square but was not chosen to play with the band.

Unfortunately I didn't pass the audition to play with the Frantic Five... Afterwards Don Lang said to me "You play well son... but I'm sorry... I've got to have you right up there in front with your music reading or it won't work well with all the acts that we get through here"... I decided to take lessons. (John Kerrison)

In the meantime Andy Mack had also heard that John had been sacked from The Episode and he invited him to join his band. They did a lot of gigs together playing at social clubs across London. The band performed covers of popular songs, for which Andy Mack wrote out the scores, including numbers such as the Beatles' 1968 hit "Lady Madonna". John recalls that when they played at London's County Hall, the offices of the now defunct "Greater London Council", he bumped into Sheila Dimmock's father who was at the time working for the GLC. After a while John's tenure playing with Andy Mack's band came to an end he was, once again, waiting for a phone call from someone who needed a drummer. Andy Mack moved to the USA a few years later and became a successful Jazz musician, both as a saxophonist and as a drummer. He worked with several famous artists including Tony Bennett, Ray Charles, Elton John, Oasis, Wet Wet Wet and Amy Winehouse.

Whilst looking for work John met up again with Johnny "Savvo" Savage", a bass guitarist who he knew from his days with the James Royal Set. Savvo had been playing alongside Mick Underwood but was now working as a plumber and John began helping him out. One day they stopped off at the Southall Community Centre where John had rehearsed with The Pirates. When he joined Episode Six he had suggested hiring the rehearsal rooms there and after he was sacked the band continued to use the centre to rehearse. John was curious as to how Mick Underwood would sound playing with the band, it sounded pretty much the same to him as when he had played with the band. The Episode continued to attract critical acclaim and John must have had some regrets that he had missed a chance for fame and fortune. However, not long afterwards both Ian Gillan and Roger Glover left the band to join Deep Purple. When Mick Underwood left to form Heavy Rock band "Quatermass" the chance of The Episode still making it big quickly faded. Subsequently The Episode returned to Beirut to exploit their established popularity and played with several changes in the line-up.

Episode Six played too many covers and not enough original material. The band managed to perform every style of music in the charts and it only worked so well because both Ian Gillan and Sheila Dimmock were such good singers. Ian in particular had an amazing voice, not just Rock stuff... they even had him singing Sandie Shaw's "Always something there to remind me" and "Island in the sun" by Harry Belafonte... Ian has an incredible vocal range. (John Kerrison)

Subsequently Johnny Savage suggested to John that they should try to put their own band together. They got hold of a very good keyboard player called Billy Davidson who worked in Joan Watson's music shop in Ealing. Billy had ginger hair and in addition to his talents on the Hammond organ he was well known for his bizarre reckless behaviour. When it came to drugs he was like a rat in a research laboratory, he would take any form of narcotic on offer. Furthermore, he would readily

113

take on any dare without any regard to the potential consequences and appeared to be totally unafraid of anything or anybody.

The trio were hired as a backing band for a Jazz singer and they rehearsed in the studios at Harlesden. John enjoyed being back in the music business and he recalls that one day, during a practice session, he met Clyde McPhatter. The vocalist was an original founder member of the American group called "The Drifters" before becoming a solo artist. Clyde had recently moved to England and meeting one of Rock & Roll's legends was a memorable experience for John. Despite rubbing shoulders with the stars the Jazz band did not get any bookings and after a short while it all just fizzled out without them ever playing any paying gigs.

After adding a guitarist to their line-up John's group passed an audition to be the backing band for "The Flirtations". The "Supremes" style all girl group from the USA had recently scored a hit with their single "Nothing but a heartache". After some rehearsals the band only performed one gig with The Flirtations. The lead guitarist was caught using drugs and, fearing repercussions concerning bad publicity if the press got hold of the story, the entire band was sacked. Subsequently The Flirtations were booked as the support act for singing superstar Tom Jones who was about to embark on a huge European tour. John had narrowly missed yet another big opportunity, his chances of getting his picture on the front page of the Melody Maker were looking slim.

John remembered the advice given to him by Mr Fairweather, his ex-girl friend's father, and decided to learn a trade that he could rely on to provide a steady income when he was "resting" between bands. Subsequently he signed up for a six month carpentry and joinery course on a "GTS" Government Training Scheme in Perivale. He had been taught the basics in woodwork classes at school plus he had also learned a great deal from his father and from working alongside Jack Rawlings in the joinery shop; this background helped him to excel on the training course. John did so well that he was often called upon to assist the instructors with teaching his fellow students the techniques that he had mastered, they said that he would be a foreman one day. After finishing the course John was soon working full-time as a qualified joiner.

I used to phone Linda every day from a telephone box. I can remember coming out of the Government Training Course with a couple of tanners (pre-decimalisation 6d coins) *to put in the phone.* (John Kerrison)

A short while later John began working in the Aintry Structures joinery shop at Hanwell with Jack Rawlings again. He enjoyed the work and he was earning good money, but it was no substitute for touring with a Rock band like Episode Six. His commitment to making it as a professional drummer was as strong as ever. In 1968 the music scene was exploding into Heavy Rock led by bands like Deep Purple and John was determined to be part of it. One possible route to the upper echelons of the music business open to him was to become a session musician working in a recording studio.

At that time there was steady work available for top drummers in the many recording studios in and around London plus minimum rates of pay were enforced by the Musicians' Union. John was an ideal candidate for such session work, after being tutored by Jim Marshall he had played with a wide variety of bands encompassing most musical styles and genres. Furthermore, he had gained valuable experience of working in several recording and rehearsal studios. In addition he was also arrogant enough to believe that he could play at the high level of proficiency required from professional session musicians.

However, both Ken Mackintosh and Don Lang had criticised John's ability to play from sheet music, a skill which was very much a requisite of studio work. Jim Marshall had tutored him on the subject of musical notation but after turning professional John rarely performed using any written arrangements. He decided that he needed lessons to brush up on his skills and one day, whilst Jack wasn't looking, he used the firm's telephone to contact Drum City to find out if there were any music teachers in his area. Subsequently he located a local drummer called John Taylor who played with a big swing band in the 1950s after having studied music during military service. He was a resident tutor at the famous Footes music shop in London for several years and he also played at the tea dances held in the Savoy Hotel. John Taylor was a nice man and he helped John swot up on his knowledge of reading music.

Chapter Fourteen

When I was young I thought that I was the dog's bollocks... I was determined to make it as a drummer. Then I got married and I had to go out to work again... I came down to earth with a great big bump... quite literally. (John Kerrison)

Drummers with John's ability and experience rarely stay idle for long and he was often called upon to play in various different bands, deputising when their usual drummer was unavailable. One day he got a telephone call from The Beachcombers who asked him to do a gig at the RAF base at Uxbridge. The important wartime air defence command centre has since been demolished and, although it is now a large housing estate, the so called "Battle of Britain Bunker" underground war rooms have been preserved. The band liked the way that John played and asked him to join on a permanent basis, he readily accepted their offer. He had known the band from back in the days when his friend Keith Moon was their drummer. The only original member left from those early times was guitarist and singer Norman Mitchener, he and John soon became close friends.

The Beachcombers got a lot of big gigs and for John it meant that, although he wasn't touring and cutting records in a recording studio, he was at least a semi-professional musician again. However, it was hard work gigging two or three times a week with the band and still holding down his job as a joiner. In addition to Norman Mitchener The Beachcombers' line-up included Clive Morgan on keyboards, John Hammond on bass guitar and vocalist Chris Luke. A short while after John joined the band Clive Morgan left, planning to go to the USA, and he was replaced by keyboard player Paul Myerson. Then Paul took over from John Hammond on bass guitar and brought in his friend Johnny Ellis to play the keyboards. John had an old battered Ford Thames van and he would drive home in the evenings after work, put his tools away in the shed, take out his drum kit and drive to the gig.

The band played covers of the popular songs in the charts encompassing Rock & Roll, Soul and Heavy Rock numbers; this included tracks recorded by bands such as Deep Purple, Blood Sweat and Tears, Led Zeppelin and Chicago. All of the band members were experienced musicians and together they earned a reputation which got them bookings to play at several classy dinner dance gigs, including some prestigious venues such as the Dorchester and the Café Royal. When England played France at rugby there was a big dinner dance held afterwards in the Rainbow Rooms restaurant, situated above the Derry & Toms department store in Knightsbridge. The Beachcombers performed at the glamorous function and John recalls being shocked by the size of the gigantic forwards who played in the French rugby team's front row.

John was still in regular contact with Linda but she was becoming increasingly dissatisfied with their long distance relationship. She gave him an "ultimatum" that either they got married or they finished altogether and John eventually agreed to wed her. Linda lived with her mother and father in a back-to-back terraced house in Salford, her parents were very much in favour of the marriage and extremely supportive. John remembers them as being nice ordinary working class people. He was also still living at home with his parents who were predictably just as supportive as his prospective in-laws. However, John's mother added a cautionary codicil to her congratulations; she told her son to make sure that he knew what he was doing. John's father reacted to news of the wedding in his usual laid back style.

In order to raise some funds for the impending nuptials John decided to sell off some of his gear. This included one of the pair of bass drums which he had purchased when he joined Episode Six. In addition he sold the drum pedal equipment and an extra tom-tom. Although he did not ever use both bass drums whilst playing with The Beachcombers John was nevertheless reluctant to sell the surplus bass drum. Perhaps he had not entirely abandoned the idea of mastering the twin bass drum format in the future, especially as it was fast becoming a popular style amongst many Heavy Rock drummers at that time.

The couple got married in 1969, around two years after they first met whilst on holiday in Greece; John was still only twenty-one years old. His best man was a motor mechanic called Peter Veryard who he had been in the year below John at school, in the same class as his brother in law Chris Whitby. John and Peter got together out of a mutual love of Mod fashion and customised scooters. In his role as best man Peter had borrowed a flashy two-tone Ford Sunliner convertible to drive John to the church ceremony in Salford. The roof on the huge American car folded back into the boot powered by an electric motor, a feature which Peter demonstrated to onlookers at every available opportunity.

It was a long drive to Salford and John, in a bout of the traditional prenuptial nervousness experienced by most bridegrooms, began having doubts about whether or not he was doing the right thing. When they took a break at a motorway service station on the M1 Peter teased him by asking if he wanted to forget about the wedding and go back to London. John gave the matter some serious consideration but in the end he decided that they had to go on. He was fully committed to marrying Linda and, with so many of his family and friends due to attend the wedding, he didn't want to let everyone down. The honeymoon consisted of a one night stay in a Manchester hotel before the newly-weds headed for their new life together in London.

At first they moved into John's parents' house at Botwell Common Road Hayes, sleeping in John's old bedroom and sharing his single bed. When they were joined later by Linda's toddler son Simon it became even more crowded in the small bedroom. John's sisters shared a larger bedroom so when Barbara got married and left home he and Linda swopped bedrooms with his older sister Annette. It was still an unsatisfactory arrangement and John applied for a council house, but he received no response. Annette had a friend whose brother was an estate agent and he found the couple a furnished flat in Ruislip Manor. The rent was a rather expensive twenty-five pounds a month, a sum which was only made affordable by virtue of John's well paid work as a joiner and his additional earnings from drumming at gigs. In a further act of commitment John officially adopted Simon who was by then about eighteen months old.

A short while later Hillingdon Council wrote and offered John and Linda a newly built flat in Cranford Drive. The couple moved in straightaway and they had to beg, borrow and steal in order to furnish the first floor maisonette. John got hold of a fridge which had a broken compressor and his friend Norman Mitchener from The Beachcombers managed to get it repaired where he worked. A few pieces of furniture were donated by John's mother and they bought a couple of wardrobes on hire purchase, fortunately the flat was already decorated. John obtained a piece of old carpet and laid it on the stairs as best as he could. He discovered that his talents did not extend to being a carpet fitter but in the end he managed to make a fairly decent job of it.

Linda got a job with the Avis car hire company in Hayes and a lady called Shirley, who conveniently lived just across the road, looked after Simon when Linda was at work. Married life was idyllic at first and John soon started to bond with his stepson who called him "Dad". He took his newfound responsibilities seriously and went out to work to support his ready made family. There was plenty of highly paid employment to be had on the building sites locally and John developed a reputation as a flash young carpenter who could be relied upon to take on even the most difficult projects. Much of the work was cash in hand with no deductions for Income Tax or National Insurance, a situation which was widespread at that time and known colloquially as working on the "Lump". As a self-employed craftsman John meticulously paid his own Class 2 National Insurance weekly stamp.

In the summer Linda's parents booked a holiday cottage in the Welsh seaside resort of Rhyl. The rented cottage included the use of a caravan in the back garden which was set aside to be used by John, Linda and Simon plus Linda's eleven year old sister. John drove there and back in his Ford Thames van, it was a good holiday and everyone enjoyed themselves. John has another fond memory from that time when, during the harsh winter, he was working for an office supplies company called "Ryman". It had become unbearably cold working on the building sites and he got a job as a delivery driver through his brother in law Chris Whitby who was the warehouse deputy manager. He took Simon out once with him on a Saturday morning in the van doing some deliveries and, when it was time for a

119

break, they went to a transport cafe in Lady Margaret Road in Southall where they had a slap-up meal. It is only a small recollection from John's past but nevertheless he still treasures it.

When the engine in the Ford Thames van seized up John bought a Vauxhall Victor estate, it was a complete rust bucket but it ran well and was large enough to transport his drum kit. Following that John purchased a Russian car called a "Volga" which had originally been owned by the Russian Embassy in London. It cost seventy-five pounds and John borrowed the money from his friend Norman Mitchener in order to buy the unusual limousine. John liked the car because it fitted his image as a Rock & Roll drummer.

At one point John worked on a project fitting out a new office block development in Feltham. He was hanging pairs of hardwood double doors when the site manager told him to stop what he was doing. When John asked if he had done something wrong the man said that he was too good for the job and sent him on to complete another contract, based in High Wycombe, which would more fully utilise his skills. He was paired up with an older joiner, ten years John's senior, who arranged to pick him up and drive him to the new job.

The task that they were given was to panel out a prestigious office with expensive exotic timbers including ash veneer boards which were fluted. John enjoyed the challenge and added extra features including a drawer and some other "master class" touches. His older companion appeared to possess far less technical ability and, despite his seniority, he constantly sought John's advice. In addition he also questioned the need to complete the work to such a high standard and with so much attention to detail. In the end John could stand no more, he picked up his tools and caught the bus home.

John had a similar experience when he was working at Heathrow Airport on the extension to the buildings at Terminal Three. He was criticised for not adhering to the plans even though his finished article corrected an obvious flaw in the original design. Like most craftsmen John found the idea of creating a substandard finish completely abhorrent and he walked off the site. Fortunately there were plenty of contractors who appreciated quality work and John was soon employed elsewhere. Whilst he was working at another site at Heathrow Airport, on a contract fitting seats and doors at the Eurobus hanger, he bumped into a man called Terry Short who he used to know when he was a teenager; in those days Terry used to play the acoustic guitar. The pair of joiners became good friends and they subsequently ended up working together.

These days John is still very willing to voice his critical opinion whenever he sees poor workmanship taking place. When his local grocery shop was recently undergoing a drastic renovation he berated and harangued the unfortunate fitters whose work he judged as being shoddy.

There's a shop front in Hillingdon that I fitted with Jack Rawlings in 1969. It was a sweet shop in those days but nowadays it's a funeral directors. When I drive past there I'm still very proud of the job that we did on it. (John Kerrison)

John rarely put in any overtime at work because he had other things to do. He was usually on piece work, whereby he was paid for the work done rather than on the hours that he worked, and he often left work mid afternoon after earning his target of ten pounds for the day. This situation gave him the flexibility to go home and change in readiness for a gig in the evenings with The Beachcombers. Whilst John was reasonably content at being a semi-professional musician it was not what he wanted, he still had dreams of achieving stardom as a Rock & Roll drummer. It was an ambition that he had steadfastly maintained since the days when he was still a schoolboy and using a biscuit tin as an improvised snare drum. With a family to support any attempt by John to return to drumming on a full-time basis would require very careful consideration.

An opportunity arose when, in May 1971, John was asked to join a newly formed band which had the potential to be signed up on a recording contract and go on tour. He was contacted by vocalist Alan Barratt and guitarist George Williams. John had known Alan since they were both about eleven years old; Alan had scored a hat trick when he played for Yeading Juniors in an eleven nil defeat of John's primary school team. John had known George Williams since he was fourteen. The band practised together in rehearsal rooms near Heathrow Airport on a Sunday. It was another chance for John to give up working as a joiner and hit the road again on tour as a Rock drummer. In the meantime he still needed to make a living.

On the following Monday morning he was back at work fitting Crittall windows on a building site in Maxwell Road Northwood. The scaffolding collapsed and John was seriously injured. Afterwards everything changed completely.

Part III - After the Accident

Chapter Fifteen

I wasn't anything anymore... I wasn't a husband, I wasn't a father, I wasn't a carpenter, I wasn't a drummer... I was just a nothing sat around all day on four wheels. I didn't really express those feelings to the doctors, the nurses, my family and my friends, or anybody else at that time. (John Kerrison)

Following his traumatic accident John spent six months in Stoke Mandeville Hospital until he was eventually discharged from the Spinal Injuries Unit on Christmas Eve in 1971. Unable to return home because of his marital difficulties he went to live with his parents at 50 Botwell Common Road in Hayes Middlesex. Despite this being the house where he was born, where he had spent an idyllic childhood and learned to play the drums, it was far from being a homecoming that he wished to celebrate. John had to be lifted through the front door because the steps prevented him from entering on his wheelchair unaided. Furthermore, he was unable to regain possession of his old bedroom upstairs due to the insurmountable barrier presented by the staircase.

It was all a bit patronising at first. My family and my friends were embarrassed to see me as I was... People were very awkward with the situation. Mum and dad had a little Jack Russell terrier called Beth... she was wonderful... she could sense that there was something wrong with me and she tried to comfort me. (John Kerrison)

In common with many working-class homes at that time the front room in the Kerrison household was set aside and kept for "best". Neatly decorated and furnished with a quality three-piece suite it was normally only used for entertaining guests on special occasions. As a temporary measure it was decided that John should sleep in the hallowed front room, using the settee as his bed at night. He had hated every minute of his stay at Stoke Mandeville but at least the hospital ward was equipped and staffed to deal with the clinical issues associated with his spinal injury. John had received no counselling whatsoever on how to cope mentally with the trauma of becoming disabled and only minimum training on how to live an independent life. He relied heavily on his mother for whom it must surely have been like having to nurse a rather large and very demanding child. Initially, in the near total absence of any constructive support, John and his mother had to learn by trial and error how to best cope with the situation.

As soon as I came home I felt that I was like a nobody, an absolutely nobody... I would not sit in the wheelchair... I hated being seen in the wheelchair and I rarely sat in it. (John Kerrison)

Shortly after arriving home John began to experience sharp pains in his abdomen, such uncontrollable muscle spasms are a typical consequence following spinal injury. His mother prepared a hot water bottle and placed it on his navel in order to help alleviate the excruciating discomfort. At first the warmth proved to be quite beneficial but when the rubber hot water bottle was removed it left behind what appeared to be a small patch of grease on John's skin. As a result of his paralysis John could not feel any sensation below his midriff and, without experiencing any pain from the heat, he had been quite badly scalded. Such incidents are a constant danger following spinal injury. Sitting too close to the fire can inadvertently lead to severe burns which the victim only becomes aware of when they begin to smell the odour of their own roasting flesh, a truly alarming experience.

When I came out of hospital there was a load of despair, a load of shut off time, a load of depression and a load of time just stuck in bed before I went out anywhere… I gave up… It was like that for about four years. (John Kerrison)

By the time that all of the festive Christmas decorations had been cleared away after the New Year celebrations any optimism concerning a reconciliation between John and his wife had waned completely. John's friend and fellow Beachcombers' band member Norman Mitchener had attempted to patch things up between the young married couple without success. When it became apparent that John would be living with his parents on a long term basis he moved to the back room and, in order to provide him with a comfortable replacement for the settee, his bed was brought down from his old bedroom. After being discharged from Stoke Mandeville Hospital John still had to make regular visits to the Spinal Injuries Unit for check ups concerning his kidney function.

I hated going back to Stoke Mandeville… I was scared in case the tests might discover something else wrong with me, something serious which they hadn't found already, because I didn't want to ever stay there again. (John Kerrison)

A month or so after moving home John began going to Hillingdon Hospital four times a week for physiotherapy and occupational therapy, transported there and back by ambulance. In the mornings he exercised in the Physiotherapy Department's gymnasium doing exercises involving bending and stretching, their were also weights and parallel bars. Dr Sperrin was in charge of the treatment sessions and at first John did not get on with him at all well. One day John realised that the doctor and his team were discussing his case without including him, even though he was nearby, and he objected. His outburst apparently cleared the air and subsequently his relationship with the physician was much improved.

Sometimes I just didn't want to go for physio… I got to know the ambulance men, they would come in when I was still in bed and say to me "Come on you lazy git, get up out of bed and come and do some work". (John Kerrison)

John would be given lunch at the hospital followed by an occupational therapy session in the afternoon. The tasks set for the patients were intended as preparation for a return to paid employment. John usually spent his time cutting up pieces of wood or modelling with plasticine. It was fairly uninspiring stuff, especially for someone who had previously worked as a skilled carpenter and had always held the sole ambition to be a Rock & Roll drummer. At first John still held some small hope, an expectation of perhaps some partial recovery from his paralysis, but he soon realised that his condition was permanent. He sank further and further into a near constant deep depression.

A couple of years after the accident I was having physiotherapy along with a guy who had suffered severe head injuries. He didn't really know what he was doing and he used to keep grabbing the physiotherapist's bum. The physio was called Janice and she was lovely. She told me that just because the other guy was grabbing her bum it didn't mean that I was allowed to do the same thing. (John Kerrison)

John had disliked the military style nursing regime which he had experienced during his stay on the Spinal Injuries Ward at Stoke Mandeville Hospital, he interpreted the brusque attitude shown by many of the medical staff as a lack of empathy. He received a similar lack of understanding from those who were charged with his medical welfare after he began living at home. There was a district nurse who visited him about once a week and although she was about the same age as John's mother her attitude was far from maternal. Most of the time she was cold and very clinical, telling John what to do whilst showing very little comprehension of what he was going through, she rarely asked what he thought was best for him. Her perfunctory efforts at nursing appear to have centred on lecturing John about the need to drink more fluids and she demonstrated no interest in his mental condition whatsoever. Over the next few years her visits dwindled and most of John's nursing requirements were more ably taken care of by his doting mother.

It's very important to have good foot care when there is no feeling in your feet. The chiropodist who used to come around to see me was a devout Jehovah's Witness. She used to drive me mad by preaching sermons while she cut my toe nails... I've never had any religious belief myself, but I understand how some people find great comfort in their faith. (John Kerrison)

The only medical person to make any attempt to treat John's deteriorating mental condition was his local GP. However, Dr Blair rarely visited his patient and the only therapy that he prescribed was in the form of antidepressant tablets. John's father had to visit the surgery to pick up the repeat prescriptions which were issued without any updated diagnosis. The pills made John sleep for most of the day and it would often be later than 3.00 pm in the afternoon before he got out of bed to get washed and dressed. Even when he did get up he just spent hours watching the television without really paying attention. After a few months John decided to stop taking the medication and he soon found another less legal way of blotting out the depressing thoughts circulating in his mind.

His "alternative" medicament was supplied by a friend who had moved to Munich and, on regular trips back to England, he kept John well supplied with large lumps of cannabis resin. John had frequently smoked dope before the accident, using it on a recreational basis. He now relied on the narcotic to help him escape the demons in his mind which were too horrific for him to face. John used the drug straight, without any tobacco, smoking it in a big curved Dunhill pipe in addition to the forty cigarettes that he got through every day. Late at night after his parents had gone to bed he would get stoned "completely off his head" whilst listening to music or watching television. His parents probably knew what he was doing because of the telltale odour coming from his room, but they never mentioned it.

I felt useless... I felt like I didn't exist... I felt just like a Tin Man, as if I was empty. I didn't go out... I was in my own world trying to get my head around my situation. I was very bitter and very angry. I didn't feel included, I felt totally excluded... now and again I still feel that way. (John Kerrison)

The only outward sign resulting from John's accident was a lump poking out from his back where his damaged vertebrae had become calcified. He developed some pressure sores which proved difficult to cure but a much more serious disorder was his state of mind. The sheer boredom of his existence allowed him to dwell upon the circumstances surrounding the accident which had left him paralysed and taken so much from his life. He was very bitter and, in the absence of any other form of release, he misdirected his anger towards his mother and to a lesser extent his father. On occasion he behaved with less maturity than a recalcitrant child.

The apparent lack of gratitude shown by John, despite the enormous support that his parents had given him, is not at all unusual following devastating events such as spinal injury. The 1989 film *"Born on the Fourth of July"* is based upon the autobiography of Ron Kovic, a US Marine who was left paralysed from the chest down following battle injuries which he received in Vietnam. The scenes in which he is portrayed by Tom Cruise behaving in an irrational and aggressive manner towards his family after returning home are very memorable. The film illustrates the painful long term mental trauma experienced by many of those who have incurred such life changing physical damage.

Although John was completely aware of what he was doing he found that he could not control himself. His truculent outbursts were always verbal and never resulted in physical violence. Prior to the accident such antagonism within the close knit and loving Kerrison family would have been unthinkable. The injury to his spine had changed John and he loathed the disagreeable person that he had become. Furthermore, the conscious recognition of his own ingratitude and the typical forgiving tolerance shown in return only served to make the situation even more distressing and painful. Although he subsequently apologised to his parents the memory of his behaviour at that time still causes him great emotional agony many years later.

My mother said to me "John, if could cut my legs off and give them to you I would, but I can't... so there it is". (John Kerrison)

In the depths of depression and despair the concept that there are those who are "worse off than yourself" has no consolation value whatsoever. Furthermore, comparisons with people who would "swap places at the drop of a hat" are equally meaningless. John's uncle said something to him one day, almost certainly without any intended malice, along the lines of "you're doing all right aren't you?". In the circumstances it was a particularly thoughtless and insensitive comment to make. At the time John was ready to bite the head off anyone, with little or no provocation, and somewhat predictably there was a huge row. It was quite some time before they spoke to each other, but eventually they made up and became "family" again.

One of my relatives had an accident and hurt his back. Fortunately there was no permanent damage to his spinal cord and he made a good recovery. He went and accused me of not trying hard enough... as if any effort would repair the lesion in my spinal cord. (John Kerrison)

In an attempt to fill the void in his life and escape the boredom that engulfed him John made a couple of half hearted attempts to start playing the drums again. He found that he had retained his talent to play a snare drum but without the use of his legs he could not achieve what he wanted musically; he had to be a "complete" drummer or not at all. After giving up on the drums he bought a xylophone. However, he soon found that he could not muster any enthusiasm for playing a different percussion instrument and so he sold it. A similar fate befell the electric organ that he purchased and tried to teach himself to play. The failure increased John's feelings of low self-worth and he soon retreated back into himself, returning to his self imposed and self damaging isolation.

It was as if I had changed into someone else, I wasn't "me" anymore. I tried but I found it impossible to take it all on board. I didn't want people to see this other person that I had become. (John Kerrison)

When John was a twelve year old schoolboy he had made a snare drum from a biscuit tin and some wallpaper, it was always his ambition to be a Rock & Roll drummer; that dream was shattered when he became paralysed. He had also lost his wife, his adopted stepson and the home that they had made together. Always completely extrovert and arrogant he had been boastful about his abilities both as a drummer and as a joiner, the accident left him with very little to brag about. This wasn't at all Rock & Roll. It often entered John's mind that perhaps it would have been better if he had met with the same terminal destiny which befell so many of his Rock contemporaries in that era.

My sister Barbara once said to me that if it had not been for the accident I would probably be dead by now... she said that the drugs and the fast driving would have got me for certain. (John Kerrison)

There was a lot happening in the music scene at that time and John kept in touch by reading the Melody Maker music newspaper, he also watched the Old Grey Whistle Test Rock programme on BBC 2 television. In 1972 he bought a new stereo system from Seven Oaks Hi Fi for a modest sum of around forty pounds; it consisted of a Garrard SP35 record deck with an amplifier and two small speakers. John built up a fairly extensive collection of vinyl LP records which he listened to throughout the day whilst chain smoking cigarettes. In the evenings he used headphones, so as not to disturb his parents, as he sat up in bed smoking dope.

Before the accident I found it difficult to cope with seeing handicapped people... so how could I cope with being seen like that myself? My friends were always trying to get me to do things but I always used to duck out of it. I had no confidence whatsoever. (John Kerrison)

John showed almost complete disinterest in taking legal action to identify any negligence contributing to his accident and secure compensation for the life-changing injuries that he had sustained. One of his friend's consulted a local solicitor on his behalf to handle both the industrial injury claim and the matrimonial divorce litigation. John knew the legal advisor working on his case because his eldest sister Annette had gone out on a date with him some years beforehand. Despite the importance of the ongoing lawsuits John took very little part in the proceedings, he paid scant attention when his solicitor spoke to him and he signed whatever documents which required his signature without even reading them.

Despite not receiving any compensation payments for the injuries that he had incurred John did not suffer any severe financial hardship. He qualified for payments of Industrial Injuries Benefits immediately after the accident by virtue of his having paid Class 2 National Insurance stamps whilst he had been working. However, there was no "lifetime pass" issued to him and, despite the permanent severity of his spinal injury, regular medical examinations were made in case there had been a reversal in his condition.

I used to get an old boy, a doctor who was in his seventies, who would regularly come to the house and assess me... It was just to see if I had had done a "Lazarus" turn and got better or if I was cheating... Did they think that a miracle might have happened? It was a complete joke. (John Kerrison)

There would often be children running around in the Kerrison household, especially when John's sister Barbara began leaving her infants in the care of her mother while she went to work. John was fond of his nephew and two nieces but they reminded him of his stepson Simon who he rarely saw because of his continuing marital difficulties. Visits from John's friends who were professional musicians also invoked mixed feelings. Whilst he was pleased to see them he was also reminded of his broken dream of being a successful Rock drummer. Regular visitors included Nick Simper (the ex Deep Purple bass guitarist was now playing with Heavy Rock band "Warhorse"), Steve Hargreaves and Chris Jackson (from The Casuals) plus Norman Mitchener and Paul Myerson (from The Beachcombers).

131

John spent most of the time alone in his room and, shut away in his own self imposed isolation, rarely ventured outdoors. His hatred for being seen in a wheelchair is by no means unique amongst those sharing his incapacity. "FDR" Roosevelt became paralysed from the waist down several years before he was elected President of the USA. The highly respected statesman went to great lengths to hide the fact that he was a paraplegic, in the firm belief that it would drastically harm his political career if his disability was ever made public. Roosevelt often wore leg callipers which enabled him to walk when he was campaigning and there are very few photographs of him in a wheelchair.

Chapter Sixteen

It was a lady called Mrs Jean Hall who was the chief occupational therapist at Hillingdon Borough Council ... she was a diamond... if it wasn't for her I would probably be dead by now.
(John Kerrison)

John had always been quite skinny but his legs became even thinner after the muscles started to waste away as a result of his paralysis. This provided less padding for the bones pressing against his flesh, increasing the risk of developing pressure sores, especially on his backside. He had taken to sitting in his commode chair for much of the day, only using the hated wheelchair when absolutely necessary. Consequently the condition of the deep ulcers on his skin worsened and forced him to spend more time in bed. The situation began to give great cause for concern. In 1995 "Superman" actor Christopher Reeves broke his neck, between the C1 and C2 cervical vertebrae, in a horse riding accident. The movie star survived but he was left in a quadriplegic condition. Tragically he died in October 2004 as a direct result of septicaemia brought about through infected pressure sores, unfortunately an all too common cause of death in spinal injury cases.

Mrs Jean Hall the chief occupational therapist from Hillingdon Borough Council was John's saviour and a tireless campaigner on his behalf. She persisted in her efforts despite his often churlish responses to any attempts to foster his rehabilitation. Jean was very concerned about John's pressure sores and, about a year after he moved into his parents' house, her research on the subject discovered a special cushion which was developed and manufactured in the USA by a company called "Debbonair". The blue cushion was made from a "Polygel" material which represented a medical breakthrough in the treatment of pressure sores, in John's case it was quite literally a "lifesaver".

Jean Hall also managed to get the council to fund the cushion's considerable purchase price of three hundred pounds. To put the cost into financial perspective it should be noted that a brand new British Leyland Mini was on sale for around six hundred pounds at that time. Currently several different types of such cushions are available, each tailored for specific situations, and John favours a model manufactured by "Jay". A highly successful cushion commonly used by quadriplegic people employs finger like projections which spread the person's weight in order to prevent damage to the skin and underlying tissue. Such technology, much of which originates from the space exploration industry, has done a great deal to drastically reduce the numbers of people dying from infected pressure sores.

The council had offered to move John and his family to a specially adapted flat shortly before he was due to be discharged from the Spinal Injuries Unit at Stoke Mandeville Hospital. Linda had kept the offer of rehousing a secret at first and, after she decided that the marriage was over, it all became irrelevant when John moved into his parents' house. The housing department deemed that the unconverted back room was suitable for John's needs and felt that they were under no obligation to relocate him into more suitable accommodation. Jean Hall refused to accept the situation, she could see how John's totally inadequate living conditions were inhibiting his rehabilitation and contributing to his clinical depression; she badgered the council on his behalf and eventually they backed down. The housing department agreed to fund the adaptations to the house which would assist John in his day to day requirements. Converting the back room by building an extension was a much more economical option than attempting to rehouse him elsewhere.

John had been living with his parents for more than a year before the building work was carried out. The housing department arranged for everything because it was a council property. The borough architect drew up the plans and they brought in their own contractor to do the work. John and his family were allowed to contribute very little of their own ideas into the project. A large temporary hoarding was put up in the back room to keep out the elements whilst the external wall was demolished and a small extension built out into the garden at the rear of the house. With no practical alternative available John remained where he was, living in the middle of a building site, enduring the additional trauma and intrusion.

It took a considerable amount of time to complete the building work and add a bathroom, much longer than was necessary in John's opinion. A pair of French doors gave him access to the back garden in his wheelchair which also made it much easier for him to leave the house. However, the overall design and the quality of the workmanship was very poor. The bathroom was fitted with a shower and toilet, complete with transfer handrails, but there was no wash basin and as a result John had to shave in the kitchen sink. The French doors were very difficult to open in a wheelchair, a standard door plus an extra "leaf" door opening on the other side would have been much more manageable. Furthermore the bolts were thoughtlessly fitted at the top of the doors which put them out of John's reach. Nevertheless it was still a big improvement in his living conditions.

At mum's house I wasn't that independent and, to a certain extent, I conceded to it all... I sort of gave in. That was until I got my head in order and it took a little while... It didn't really start until we got the extension done and that's when I started moving forward a bit more. (John Kerrison)

After the building work was completed John was still loathe to leave the back room at his parents' house and, whenever he did venture into the outside world, he still hated being seen in his wheelchair. If he saw a photograph which showed him sitting in a wheelchair it made him feel sick. He was therefore very apprehensive when Derek Radburn, one of the friends that he grew up with in Botwell Common Road, managed to coax him into going out for a Sunday lunchtime drink. They went to a pub called "The Music Box" in Derek's van but, although there was live music being played, John was not at all comfortable with being seen in his wheelchair and he did not enjoy the experience.

A short while later John heard from Clive Morgan who was about to go and live in the USA. The former keyboard player in The Beachcombers was throwing a reunion party for all the musicians

135

who had ever played in the band all the way back to the 1960s. John felt particularly awkward at the party, he was very self-conscious about being in a wheelchair in front of his former colleagues. The situation was made even more difficult because, through embarrassment or misplaced politeness, everyone avoided talking about John's accident. The atmosphere at the party did not stay sombre and reserved for very long once Keith Moon had arrived. John and Keith had been friends since they met as young teenagers in Jim Marshall's music shop, both drummers had played with The Beachcombers. "Moon the Loon" drank a whole bottle of brandy and he was soon up to the sort of madcap antics which made him a Rock & Roll legend.

Moony took one look at me in my wheelchair and shouted "John, what the **** happened to you?"... I told him all about it. (John Kerrison)

The ever supportive Jean Hall also informed the Social Services Department about John's circumstances and they assigned a case worker called Ann Powell to assist him. Ann became a regular visitor at the Kerrison's house, she and John soon became good friends. Under her counselling he began to understand the process that he was going through following the trauma of losing the use of his legs, in many ways it was similar to grieving. The social worker gave John a book to read which helped him to try and put everything into perspective.

There's a book by Peter Maris called "Loss and change". It's a sociology book and it's about people being moved forcibly from their homeland to somewhere else. There is hate, there is bitterness, there is rejection and anger. It's all about trying to go from loss to change... adapting. (John Kerrison)

Although John never actually went to court himself about the accident he did attend a legal hearing in Slough concerning obtaining access to see Simon. It was about three years after he and Linda had split up and there was still a great deal of ill feeling between them, as a result sometimes John was not allowed to see his stepson. Linda failed to put in an appearance at the custody hearing and a prescribed order was issued by the court which allowed John to see Simon once every two weeks.

After I got married Simon and me did bond in a way at first, but after the accident it was very difficult when I had to fight for custody and I hadn't really got my head around being in a wheelchair... It was a bit of a hit and miss relationship... we still talk regularly on the phone and we remain good friends. (John Kerrison)

John sat isolated in the back room for about four years, passing the endless hours by listening to records, watching television and filling his head with morbid thoughts. Chain smoking cigarettes and getting stoned in the evenings was a meagre existence. There were few major incidents to provide points of reference nowadays in his memories of that time. John recalls simple things such as buying a colour television set in 1974 to watch the World Cup, even though England had disappointingly failed to qualify. Everything changed the following year when John underwent some major alterations in his mundane and soul destroying routine.

Apart from trips to receive medical treatment John rarely left his sanctuary, despite the best efforts of his family and friends. In 1975 Rodney Keen eventually persuaded him into going out for a drink at the nearby EMI Social Club, it took a great deal of pestering. Prior to the accident John had never been much of a drinker and later, even in the depths of depression, he had not sought to drown his sorrows by drinking at home. However, he began making up for lost time with a great deal of enthusiasm. As well as becoming a regular at the EMI Social Club he also went on the "LINO", Lads Inebriated Nights Out, which were organised by Paul Myerson. Soon John was going out seven nights a week binge drinking and, although he went home extremely drunk nearly every evening, his parents never said anything about it.

At first I was too scared to go out... then it was like being born again... I didn't know how the people in the club would take to me being in a wheelchair... It ended up with me getting drunk every single night of the week. There was nothing else to do. (John Kerrison)

The situation was strangely liberating whilst at the same time it was equally self destructive. One evening there was a special offer in the EMI Social Club bar, they were selling "Harvey Wall Bangers" for one pound a time; a cocktail whose primary constituent of vodka is fortified by a liberal shot of the alcohol based herbal liqueur "Galliano" and then topped up with orange juice. John drank twelve of the potent beverages and, quite unsurprisingly, he threw up. After unwisely drinking a thirteenth serving he decided that it was time to go home. He didn't bang into any walls but, whilst drunkenly navigating the path alongside his parents' house, the inevitable happened and he toppled over.

Lying helpless on the ground beside his wheelchair he was forced to shout for help, it was late at night and both his parents were in bed. Fortunately his father heard him and came to John's aid dressed in his pyjamas. Mr Kerrison senior was only about five foot five inches tall and approaching pension age but, coping with the situation in his usual laid back manner, he somehow managed to get his extremely intoxicated son back into the wheelchair. Once he was safely upright again John managed to get himself indoors and into his bed without further mishap.

Dad never had a go at me... all he said was "Are you all right son?" He must have known what I was going through... The drinking slowed down a bit eventually but it was always there in the background... perhaps not as head-on as before. (John Kerrison)

John began to feel much more relaxed about being seen in his wheelchair and he started to gain the confidence to travel further afield. He accompanied his mother and father when they went to John Harris's wedding at Hebden Bridge on the Yorkshire border. Another big step was when he went on holiday to Malta with his parents in 1976, the flight and the accommodation was booked through a travel agent in Heston. It was the first time that John had flown as a disabled passenger and it proved to be a challenging experience. He was transferred on and off the airplane, prior to the rest of the passengers, assisted by airport staff who trundled him about in a small evacuation style chair; his own standard size wheelchair was too wide to fit down the narrow aisle between the seats.

When they arrived in the coastal town of Marsaskala there was a mix up and, instead of accommodation which provided level entry, they were given an apartment which was on the first floor. The people who had been given the correct ground floor villa uncharitably refused to swop and so John had to be carried up and down a flight of stairs every time that he ventured outside. The Kerrisons returned to Malta the following year and stayed in a place near Valetta, this time they took Simon with them. It was close to the peak temperatures of the roasting hot Maltese summer and John did not get much chance to enjoy the holiday because he spent part of the time in bed recovering from heat stroke.

A young man called Malcolm Price was a hairdresser in the salon where John's mother got her hair done, he also cut John's hair. One day he introduced John to a district nurse called Mrs Jee. She took a real interest in John, frequently visiting him to check that he was keeping well. Using her position as a hospital sister she arranged for him to have better home care and transferred him to a different doctor's surgery. John got on well with his new GP Dr Sutton, he showed great deal more concern for his well being than any of his previous physicians. Dr Sutton was in the habit of drinking four cans of Special Brew in the evenings whilst he filled out the repeat prescriptions for his patients, he was definitely the sort of GP that John preferred. He would often invite John back to his house for dinner. These days John still attends the same surgery where he is treated by Dr Rajan who used to be Dr Sutton's partner.

John became good friends with the Jee family and one summer he went on holiday with them to the mediterranean island of Ibiza.

In Ibiza we went on one of those organised excursion where you get a meal and loads of wine. By the time it had finished I was drunk and Mr Jee was trying to hurry me up to get back on the coach. "Let him be, John has got a lot to deal with" Mrs Jee told him. She was great, she really understood what I was going through. (John Kerrison)

John often whiled away the hours reading the newspapers and periodical which his mother bought for him. One of the periodicals that he regularly perused was called the "Exchange and Mart", a weekly classified magazine which carried thousands upon thousands[of adverts offering to sell just about everything under the sun. Combing through the craft advertisements he spotted some woodworking plans for sale and, acting pretty much on impulse, he decided to purchase a set of drawings detailing how to build a long case "grandfather" clock; a particular species of timepiece which he had always wanted to own. It was obviously a very challenging long term project but, if nothing else, John had plenty of time on his hands and he had also acquired the necessary joinery skills before his accident.

John's father was also a skilled joiner and, keen to get his son doing something constructive, he enlisted help from some of the timber suppliers where he worked to source the required materials. He managed to get hold of some Brazilian mahogany, high quality cuts of "knot free" hardwood which would be very difficult and prohibitively expensive to obtain these days. The shed next to the house was set up as a workshop and John spent an hour or so every day on his new project. It was usually when he was in the depths of despair that he did most of the work, perhaps attempting to prove to himself that he was not totally useless and that there was some kind of meaningful future to his life.

He took great pride in his work and wherever possible he did everything by hand, completely forsaking the use of any power tools. However, the "swan necks" and the ornamental "pilaster" style mouldings were run out by an expert spindle turner who John had met in the EMI Social Club. When he was constructing the clock's case and waist door John forsook the usual mortice and tenon and used a more difficult example of joinery called a "fox wedge tenon" which, in a masterclass of cabinetmaking, produced a very secure joint without the end grain showing.

It was something that suited my skills. Even before the accident, when I was just a cheeky twenty-one year old, I used to get lots of work because of my skill... I was a flash git before the accident and I wanted to somehow still be like that... I wanted something that I could brag about. (John Kerrison)

John took a great deal of time constructing the clock case and when it was finished he had it French polished, he also got someone to cut a piece of glass for the clock face. The high quality German clock movement that he fitted into the case, complete with pulleys and weights, was purchased from the USA; it cost a small fortune. When the grandfather clock was complete and working John was justifiably very proud of his highly skilled handiwork. His father was full of praise but, as a very experienced joiner himself, he still managed to find a couple of minute faults. Making a grandfather clock was a very worthwhile exercise for John but it did not in any way replace the loss that he had suffered.

Part IV - Leaving Home

Chapter Seventeen

Learning to become self-sufficient after a major spinal injury isn't just about the physical practicalities... it's all about your mind set... You may know what you need to do but you just don't want to do anything... It can take a long time to get your head around it. (John Kerrison)

In 1977 John went to a party at Botwell House in Hayes which, situated in Botwell Lane, was only a short distance from his parents' house. The event was organised to raise funds for the adjacent Roman Catholic Immaculate Heart of Mary Church. In the 1960s the venue had hosted many of the major bands of that era and John had himself played there several times. It was at the charity function that he bumped into an attractive divorcee called Margaret. She was a local girl from Botwell Lane whom John had known in his youth, when he was about eighteen and she was fifteen. Her father was an Irishman whose bright and cheerful disposition had earned him the nickname "Sunny". John plucked up the courage to ask Margaret out and they dated for about nine months before he moved into her council flat in Avondale Drive Hayes.

Leaving home was a big move for John and, even though he was still less than a ten minute drive from his parents' house, he had to dig very deep psychologically to try and overcome his lack of self confidence. It was also a very brave decision on Margaret's part, she was fully aware of the challenges presented by John's disability and the huge amount of mental baggage that accompanied him.

Fortunately the flat in Avondale Drive was on the ground floor and, after John's father built a small wooden ramp outside the front door, it was accessible by wheelchair. Entry later became only slightly more difficult when the ramp began to rot away after exposure to the elements.

Margaret's maisonette had none of the alterations required to facilitate the demands of John's disability and together they had to make do with what was in place. John used to sit on the toilet to wash himself with Margaret's assistance. The situation was as basic and demanding as his parents' house had been prior to the extension being built. Leaving home represented a major move towards John achieving some sort of independence after years of total reliance on his parents and on his mother in particular. However, he still had to battle with his issues concerning his lack of self confidence and his feelings of low self worth.

In another big step John decided to take up driving again and he bought a second-hand Hillman Avenger from a garage run by his friend John Ellis, a former keyboard player in The Beachcombers. The vehicle was green in colour but a far more important feature was that it had an automatic gear box which, together with hand controls for the brake and the throttle, enabled John to drive it. A Hillman Avenger was not his preferred choice of car make or model but there were not that many affordable automatics around in those days. John had passed his driving test several years before his accident and there was no requirement for him to undergo any further examination, except for a check on his eye sight, despite his having lost the use of his legs. Immediately after buying the car John and Margaret made plans to go on a weekend trip to Stratford-upon-Avon. However, before they embarked on their journey the vehicle first had to be serviced and then adapted so that John could drive it.

The hand controls were supplied as a relatively simple kit consisting of rods and cables which, attached to the car's steering column, were operated by butterfly switches; this enabled the brake and accelerator pedals to be operated by hand. The whole assembly could be removed quite quickly and easily to allow anyone to drive the car normally. Despite the promises made by John Ellis the car was still not ready the night before John and Margaret were planning to go away. When John's father protested about the situation the mechanic, a supposed friend of the family, responded by physically pushing the older man quite hard. It was a totally unnecessary act of violence for which John has never forgiven John Ellis who has since passed away. The incident put a something of a dampener on the weekend visit to Shakespeare's birthplace.

John turned thirty on 4 August 1977 but twelve days later, on 16 August 1977, there was a much more significant date in the annals of Rock & Roll history.

I was driving in my car around Bourne Circle near Bourne Avenue, I was with Margaret and the radio was playing... that's how I heard the news that Elvis had died. I remember it really well. There was a big empty feeling... he was part of history. (John Kerrison)

Three months after moving into Margaret's home John left and went back to live in his parent's house, returning to the insulated sanctuary provided by the back room. There was no friction between them as a couple and the flat did not present any insurmountable difficulties relating to John's condition, the problem was most definitely John's mental state. Sometimes he felt self-conscious being seen in his wheelchair in the company of an attractive woman, but that was only part of his insecurity. John's feelings of low self worth, his depression and his anger robbed him of his ability to cope with being in a stable relationship. Margaret was as understanding as always and, aware of the demons that John was facing, she stayed in contact with him. Long afterwards she still continued to offer him support with no residual ill feeling concerning his sudden departure.

I chickened out... Basically I ran away back to mum's house... All of the problems were with me and not Margaret... she would do anything for me and she tried to help... she was lovely. I couldn't get my head around being in a wheelchair let alone being in a relationship. I was aware that it was all in my mind but that just made it all the more frustrating. (John Kerrison)

In the meantime John's industrial injury negligence claim was still tediously grinding its way through the archaic British legal system. John himself took little part in the process and never went to

144

see what happened in any of the court hearings. He just followed the advice of his legal advisers and signed whatever documents that they put in front of him. The case was eventually resolved in his favour and he was awarded £33,000 in compensation for his injuries. It was a somewhat paltry sum by today's standards when, in similar circumstances, six and seven figure payouts are apparently quite common.

John believes that he received a reduced payment because the income from his Industrial Disability Pension was taken into account, despite the fact that he qualified for the benefit solely by virtue of his own payments of National Insurance contributions. He does not know if anyone was prosecuted, under health and safety regulations, for the dangerous condition of the scaffolding. Whilst the compensation money gave John a certain degree of financial security it would have most certainly have been of greater benefit if it had been paid out shortly after the accident instead of nearly seven years later. In recent years the government introduced a system to streamline several types of injury claims but complex cases can still take a long time to reach a settlement.

The "disabling" professions are the doctors, lawyers and politicians. Sometimes they "disable" people more than any disability. (John Kerrison)

John's used part of his newly acquired healthy bank balance to assist his younger sister Barbara. Her husband Chris was serving a lengthy prison sentence, after being convicted of an armed robbery, despite his persistent protests that he was innocent. The case against Chris was flimsy at best, his conviction was based on circumstantial evidence and relied heavily on a positive identification by an eyewitness. Chris had been working on the night shift, pressing records at the EMI factory on the Uxbridge Road. He went home and was in bed when an armoured van delivering wages was robbed at gun point. Nevertheless he was picked out on an identity parade line-up and, after being tried at the Old Bailey, he was subsequently sent to prison. John tried to help by offering a substantial reward for information leading to his brother-in-law's release.

I had given Chris a present of a replica Colt 45 revolver which I had bought through an advert in the Exchange and Mart... I gave it to him for a laugh. A shot was fired during the robbery and apparently the prosecution tried to suggest that the replica was used, even though it couldn't be fired and it wasn't the proper metal... it was that stupid. (John Kerrison)

At that time there was a campaign being organised against the reliance solely on eyewitness identification evidence to gain convictions in court. The protests centred on a man called George Davis who, just like Chris, had also been found guilty of an armed robbery after being picked out on an identity parade. Barbara became heavily involved in the campaign which caught the attention of the public by the widespread use of "George Davis is innocent" graffiti and well reported acts of vandalism. Protesters dug up the pitch at the Headingley cricket ground prior to an England v Australia test match to attract publicity for their cause. Celebrities such as Roger Daltrey of The Who and a Labour MP rallied behind the campaign and eventually George Davis was released from prison. He was later found guilty of committing a different armed robbery and sent back to jail.

A breakthrough in Chris's case came about when he was transferred to another prison. He was approached by an inmate who, motivated by a sense of justice or the potential reward, was willing to give evidence about the people who had actually committed the payroll hold-up. After much complex legal wrangling Chris was exonerated and he was released around a year later. John is unsure how much compensation, if any at all, his brother-in-law was paid for the miscarriage of justice which resulted in his wrongful conviction. Afterwards Chris and Barbara moved out of London and, about the same time, John's eldest sister Annette left home and went to work in Libya for the oil company Exxon based in Tripoli.

John decided that he should put his own compensation money to good use and try to become more independent. He bought a three bedroom semi-detached house in Goshawk Gardens which was situated about two miles from Botwell Common Road, on the other side of the Uxbridge Road. Having failed at his first attempt to leave home John was determined to get everything right this time. The location was carefully selected, it was close enough for him to still receive support from his family and friends but, at the same time, at a sufficient distance to maintain a large degree of independence. Furthermore, the house was on a corner plot so that an extension could be built on the side for a bedroom and a bathroom, the rest of the ground floor was converted to meet John's needs. A great deal of thought was put into small things such as the positioning of the door entry phone, the light switches, the bathroom facilities, and level access to the garden.

Loose floor coverings such as rugs and fitted carpets do not mix well with wheel chairs because they can receive uneven wear from the rubber tyres, plus they have a tendency to get dragged out of position. John had learned from his own experience and he had the ground floor laid with expensive industrial quality carpet tiles which, like those used in shops and offices, are hard wearing and they can be moved around when they become damaged. The kitchen hob was fitted so that John could get his legs underneath and not have to reach forward when he was cooking. A shower cubicle was fitted in the bathroom with transfer rails for John to hold when using the toilet and the shower seat.

Leaving home proved to be a huge task and John's father was an enormous help with the conversion. When there were problems with the builders he got an apprentice bricklayer and an apprentice carpenter, who were friends of the family, to finish the job. Margaret also assisted with the move. She suggested converting the rooms upstairs which, although inaccessible to John, could provide accommodation for visitors and in case he required resident helpers. Whilst Margaret did everything that she could to help John she was adamant that she would not move in with him, no doubt she had learned a lesson from her previous experience on that subject. After everything was finished the grandfather clock which, having formed part of John's slow and continuing rehabilitation, took pride of place in his new home.

After I moved to Goshawk Gardens I again developed some quite bad pressure sores and I had to spend a long time in bed. I was very fortunate to have an extensive network of family and friends living close by who supported me at that time. (John Kerrison)

147

John soon began to socialise more and more, travelling further afield now that he was driving again. A favourite venue was the Rising Sun in Sudbury where he often went to see his ex school friend Eddie Richards, a former member of "Edison Lighthouse", playing in a band called "Heyday". The line-up included Spencer James (now with "The Searchers") and Robin Scrimshaw (who had played bass guitar in "The Flowerpot Men"). John also stopped his bouts of heavy drinking, in order to reduce the risk of suffering from repeated bladder infections, but he continued to dabble with illegal narcotics.

I used to drop half a tab of speed and drive to watch a band play at a gig where I would drink orange juice all night. Halfway through the evening I would drop the other half so that I was still sober enough to drive home. (John Kerrison)

At that time "Citizens Band" radio had become a phenomenal success and John became interested through a friend who imported illegal CB radios into the UK. John bought a combined radio and CB set whilst he was in the USA and he subsequently joined a CB club in his local area. He attended club runs in his car, going by the nickname CB user "handle" of "Ironside" and was interviewed on BBC radio about his hobby. The illegal CB communication system was also very popular amongst housebound disabled people. It kept them in touch with the outside world whilst providing anonymity concerning their condition, aiding acceptance when socialising on the air waves. John and many other CB users lost interest when it became legalised in early 1980s.

Social worker Ann Powell was not just John's case worker, she was also his friend. Ann was particularly pleased with his progress but decided that it was time for him to attempt to integrate further with the outside world. She encouraged him to become a volunteer visitor at the "Alderbourne Rehabilitation Unit" which, developed as part of Hillingdon Hospital, catered for disabled people who could not be cared for at home. John began playing table tennis regularly with a young resident called Derek Bradshaw despite his having resisted attempts to make him undertake such sporting activities as part of the therapy at Stoke Mandeville Hospital.

I used to go in there in my car every other day at that time. I could get a lunch or a cup of tea and socialise with the people there... I didn't feel so self-conscious because I had a job to do... it wasn't about the wheelchair. (John Kerrison)

Whilst working as a volunteer at the Alderbourne Rehabilitation Unit John met a remarkable man called Trevor Wells who, just like John, had also worked as a carpenter until a spinal cord injury in 1978 ended his career. Trevor had been playing rugby for the Uxbridge Rugby Club when he was in a scrum which collapsed and he broke his neck. As a tetraplegic, paralysed from the shoulders down, he lost the ability to move his arms and his legs. In hospital he taught himself to paint, with painstaking attention to detail, using a brush held in his mouth. He is now assisted by a specially designed artist's easel which he is able to move electronically. John and Trevor soon became firm friends and they remain so today.

I first met Trevor Wells in the Alderbourne Rehab Unit. He asked me if I would like a cup of tea... it was an interesting offer because he was a quadriplegic. I replied "I'd love one" and he said to me "can you make me one too?"... I liked his attitude and from that moment on we became soulmates. (John Kerrison)

Trevor's work has become very sought after and he has achieved commercial success, particularly in the field of birthday and Christmas cards. He is also a leading member of the "Mouth and Foot Painting Artists" (MFPA) who support and promote the work of artists who paint without the use of their hands. When they first met John was struck by how different Trevor was from the other residents in the Rehab Unit; he found that many disabled people were very demanding whereas Trevor showed a great deal of empathy towards him. Furthermore Trevor appeared to "park" his thoughts concerning his spinal injury and get on with his life as best as he could. This was very much in contrast to John who had constantly dwelt on his own misfortune. Trevor has been an inspiration to many disabled people.

I have seen Trevor's hand drawings of tools in his exercise books from when he was doing his carpentry apprenticeship as a teenager... they were very meticulous. When he paints now with his mouth it is also very detailed and almost photographic. (John Kerrison)

A few years after John moved to Goshawk Gardens he began to experience some really bad bouts of "UTI" urinary tract infections. He was referred for treatment at Hillingdon Hospital where he was admitted to a male wing charmingly referred to by the patients as the "Willy Ward". John was impressed by the level of nursing care that he received from the doctors and the nursing staff. The senior urologist at the hospital was a highly experienced consultant called Mr Johns. He was very kind and sympathetic towards his patients, John often went see him as a private patient but was never asked for any payment. Unfortunately Mr Johns later died of bladder cancer; ironically falling victim to a condition from his own specialist field of medicine.

Sister Maguire and her nursing staff at Hillingdon Hospital were the most empathetic medical people that I have ever met. When I was first admitted she told them "Let John get up on his own, he organises himself well at home so don't start pushing him". She treated me as a "whole" person. (John Kerrison)

Chapter Eighteen

There was an emotional loss when I was injured... I had feelings of being not wanted... I didn't feel like being wanted, because of what I had become... I felt that I was a thing, not a person. (John Kerrison)

The Golden Cross pub situated on the corner of Botwell Lane in Hayes had always been a meeting place for John plus his sisters and their friends in the 1960s, after it was knocked down and rebuilt they referred to it as the "New Cross". Following his move to Goshawk Gardens John often met up with his mates there and one evening in the early 1980s he spotted a couple of young ladies who were drinking at the end of the bar, they stood out because they were both wearing fancy dress costumes. It was less than two years after John had moved out of his parents' house and he was still quite uncomfortable about being seen in his wheelchair.

Despite his reticence John still exchanged a few awkward words with the pair of teenage girls who had stopped off at the Golden Cross for a drink on their way to a party. He was very flattered that he had been paid any attention in the chance encounter and soon discovered that his new female acquaintances were called Caroline and Debbie. It was Caroline who particularly caught his eye, not just because she was an attractive and petite red head but also because she was wearing a French maid's outfit. At a later date John met Caroline and her friend again when they paid a return visit to the pub; it was the start of a long term and close friendship.

John started going out with Caroline, usually together with her friend Debbie, picking her up in his car about once a week. They all had similar tastes in music and they would often go and see different bands play, visiting many of the local West London venues where John had himself performed before his accident. When they were together in public nobody made any derogatory comments about seeing a disabled guy going out with a pair of young ladies and Caroline was never embarrassed to be seen with him. John became less self-conscious, the wheelchair was never any kind of barrier in their relationship.

It was a bit of a breakout for me and it made me feel more included... She had only ever known me like that (in a wheelchair) and she accepted me like that. (John Kerrison)

Over the following years John and Caroline became quite close and they developed something of a mutual support system. However, he wanted much more from their relationship but his requests that that they should live together were always met with a negative response; nevertheless, they remained good friends and continued to meet regularly. John's friends said very little to him about the situation but it was fairly obvious that they did not approve.

I was included and yet, at the same time, I was also excluded from having a permanent and committed relationship... but it was nothing to do with me being in a wheelchair or even the age difference, it was a lot of other stuff that I have never really come to terms with. (John Kerrison)

Mrs Kerrison developed type II diabetes in late 1970s and over the following years the condition progressed to a chronic level. When she began to experience circulatory problems in her legs and feet, an extreme symptom of the metabolic disorder, drastic surgery was required. She endured a series of painful and traumatic operations which started with the removal of her toes followed by parts of her feet, finally culminating in the amputation of both of her legs. The progressive loss of her lower limbs prompted John's father to ask the surgeon how much of his wife he was ultimately going to leave for him. Mrs Kerrison faced the ordeal with her characteristic stoicism. John visited his mother every day and she would often crack jokes about the pair of them both being in wheelchairs.

I was the best man at a friend's wedding and my mother came to the church service. Mum said that me and her should be called "the bookends" because we were both in wheelchairs. (John Kerrison)

The Kerrison's house at 50 Botwell Common Road had been converted in order to enable John to live there after his accident and the facilities were conveniently still in place when his mother became disabled. Unable to use the stairs she moved into the back room previously occupied by her son, utilising the same bathroom equipment and the wheelchair access which had been put in place for him. John's father often used to take her out for a drive in his car with her wheelchair stowed in the boot; he had obtained an orange disabled sticker which, placed in the window of his vehicle, allowed preferential parking concessions. Beth the Jack Russell always accompanied them wherever they went.

There were removable arm rests on my wheelchair and for some reason I took one of them off and went around like that... I really don't know why. My mum started doing the same thing... when I asked her why she did it she said that she was just copying me. (John Kerrison)

On the occasion of Mr and Mrs Kerrison's 40th "ruby" wedding anniversary a hall in the Hedgewood School at Weymouth Road Hayes was hired to host a party. The venue was chosen because the school hall had adequate wheelchair access for John and his mother plus there was ample room to accommodate the many relatives and friends who attended the celebratory event. Throughout the evening Caroline and her friend Debbie worked behind the bar serving drinks. John had recruited Caroline's assistance because he wanted her to be involved as much as possible in his life.

Caroline got married in her early twenties, around four or five years after we first met... I went to her wedding and I got drunk celebrating... I had mixed emotions, I was happy for her and sad for myself... but we will always remain very good friends. (John Kerrison)

Mrs Kerrison was always a very practical woman and, realising that she did not have long to live, told John to look after his father when she was gone; her concern for her husband's welfare having increased after he was diagnosed with oesophageal cancer. On Boxing Day 1986, about eighteen months after losing her legs, Mrs Kerrison fell ill whilst at home and she was taken to the Accident and Emergency Department in an ambulance. She passed away peacefully within half an hour of arriving at the hospital. It is of great comfort to John that they had plenty of time to say goodbye to one another and discuss the situation in the months prior to her anticipated death. John's mother was always outspoken, a straight talker who meant what she said and seldom pulled her punches, a trait which he has fully inherited.

John's parents had purchased their own burial plot in advance, as was the common custom for many people of their generation; it was situated in the Shepiston Lane Cemetery in Hayes. On the day of the funeral it was pouring down with rain and John could not get close to the graveside because his wheelchair kept sinking into the soft mud. A well built friend called Russ, a muscular competitive rower, picked him up and carried him to the burial plot. He held him in his arms throughout the funeral service. The next day John noticed that his father was getting ready to venture out into the inclement weather and he asked him where he was going. His father replied jokingly that he was going to the cemetery to put an umbrella over mum's grave because she was getting wet. No matter what the circumstances humour and fun was never something absent in the close knit Kerrison family.

John's father died about eight months later in August 1987 in Harefield Hospital. The carcinoma in his oesophagus had begun to make it difficult for him to swallow food and an attempt was made to insert a tube in his throat, bypassing the tumour, to enable him to eat. He had suffered with a lung problem since his childhood, a condition which ended his military service, and it was a contributory factor when he did not survive the operation. Both of John's parents were in their seventies when they passed away. They had purchased their council house under the government's "right to buy" scheme and when they died it had to be sold back to the local authority at its market value. This was a stipulation imposed when Mr and Mrs

Kerrison bought the house due to the work which had originally been carried out to enable John to live there after his accident.

In the years that followed John continued to grow in self-confidence and, gradually tackling the demons which had haunted him since the accident, he set about coming to terms with his disability. Whilst living at Goshawk Gardens he began socialising, going to watch bands and he also took a strong interest in campaigning for issues concerning access and equality relating to the disabled. He explored the potential remedies offered by several forms of alternative medicine, with varying degrees of success. His self assurance developed and he began travelling further afield to Europe, the USA and even to Australia. However, his most important achievement was learning to play the drums again despite the paralysis in his legs, reawakening his ambition that he had held since his childhood to be a professional Rock & Roll drummer.

Before the accident the only disabled musician that I saw was a guy called Jimmy... he had a clubfoot and he wore a special boot... In the mid 1960s Jimmy played the piano in every pub in Hayes... he always had a roll-up fag in his mouth. (John Kerrison)

John had remained in regular contact with his stepson throughout the years since the accident and the subsequent less than amicable divorce from Linda. When Simon was in his mid twenties he announced that he was getting married, the service was held in a Roman Catholic church in Eccles. John went to the wedding with his eldest sister Annette. There were a large number of people from Linda's side of the family but John did not feel in anyway intimidated; he had always gotten on well with his ex wife's parents and he describes one of her brothers as being the salt of the earth. However, there was an awkward moment outside the church when Linda suddenly came up and kissed John. He had not seen her since their separation after the accident more than two decades earlier and, still harbouring a certain amount of bitterness, he did not welcome the gesture whatever the intention behind it.

Everybody has regrets in life, a missed opportunity with unknown life-changing consequences. John developed a passion for all things Italian that began as a teenager when he played in Rome with The

Eccentrics. John has often wondered as to how different his life would have been if he had stayed there. He has returned to Rome a couple of times and, as a labour of love, sometime in the mid 1990s he attended Italian language evening classes once a week for five years. He subsequently passed the GCE "A" level examination and he is particularly proud of a poem that he wrote in Italian about his love of Rome.

Roma by John Kerrison
La citta con i setti colli
The city with seven hills
Le fontane luminose con l'aqua biańca
The illuminated fountains with white water
Le strade piene di gente
The streets filled with people
Che bella cittá, si ricorda
What a beautiful city, you remember

Il Vaticano dove aspetta la gente
The Vatican where the people wait
Speranza vedere Il Papa
Hoping to see the Pope
Sfortunato oggi non, c' è
Unfortunately he's not there today
Che bella cittá, si ricorda
What a beautiful city, you remember

Gli stranieri dappertutto, da tutto il mondo
Foreigners from all over the world
Mescolano con i Romani e i moumenti
Mingle with the Romans and monuments
Gli anziani e i giovani
The elderly and the young
Che bella cittá, si ricorda
What a beautiful city, you remember

L'aeroporto e la stazione Termini
The airport and the station Termini

Da dove parte la gente
From where the people depart
Arrivederci Roma
Say goodbye to Rome
Che bella città, si ricorda
What a beautiful city, you remember

Sometime around 1996 John was readmitted to Stoke Mandeville Hospital to undergo a surgical procedure relating to a bladder pressure problem. At first he was very apprehensive about returning to the hospital, even as a short term resident, having had such a negative experience as a patient there more than two decades earlier. However, John was pleasantly surprised to find that the ethos had changed completely. There now appeared to be a great deal more empathy and respect shown by the medical staff.

There was a senior consultant at Stoke Mandeville called Mr Gardner who was very empathetic. He said to me "What can we do for you Mr Kerrison?", asking what I thought was the best for me... he may have heard about how much fuss that I could kick up when I wanted to. (John Kerrison)

One of the patients travelled up and down the ward on a strange contraption called a "prone trolley", propelling himself by pushing the wheels around just like on a standard wheelchair but lying horizontally and face down. The man seemed to spend most of the time on his own and someone said that he was Greek. John offered him a cigarette and discovered that he was in fact an Italian called Salvatore Rosselli who was a shirtmaker from the island of Sicily. Several years earlier, whilst still a teenager, he had damaged his spine in a motorcycle accident and lost the use of his legs. He was being treated for pressure sores, his unusual trolley wheelchair removed the stress on the affected areas plus it gave him both mobility and valuable exercise. Meeting Salvatore was a good opportunity for John to practise his Italian language skills.

Salvatore was a really nice guy... He invited me to stay at his house which was in a town called Casteldaccia, near Palermo, where he lived with his family. (John Kerrison)

John was about fifty years old when he started going out with a lady from Wandsworth called Susan. He met her when he went to watch his friend Nick Simper play a gig with "The Good Old Boys" at the Angler's Retreat public house in West Drayton; she was there with her friend who was dating a member of the band. After a short while they decided to set up home together and, around 1997, John moved out of Goshawk Gardens and bought a chalet bungalow in Shepperton. The Middlesex town was chosen because of the location of a specialist school which would benefit Susan's young son who suffered from a speech impediment. John's cousin had a daughter who worked at the school and assisted them in securing a place for the boy. The ground floor of the bungalow was converted at great expense, with a shower room and toilet, to accommodate John's wheelchair.

We used to call the Golden Cross pub the "New Cross" after it was rebuilt... The Good Old Boys played there and a guy in the bar called Micky Collins used to drop his kaks at some point during the evening... we used to laugh because he always had skid marks in his underpants. (John Kerrison)

Susan's brother-in-law supported Farnborough Town FC and he invited John to a home game because they were playing Hayes FC. John had supported Hayes since he was a schoolboy but later on, when he became a professional musician, he rarely had the time to go to any of their matches on a Saturday because he usually had to travel to a gig. After the accident he had ample opportunity to watch Hayes play at home because their ground was close by, only his lack of self confidence prevented him from going. When he went to the match at Farnborough a member of the Hayes team recognised him, the Australian football player had viewed John's house in Goshawk Gardens when it was up for sale. John soon felt at ease and since then he has consistently made every effort to support Hayes FC.

158

Recently I went with my mate along to see Hayes play in an away game and we sat near the home team's dugout. A man got out of the dugout and said to me "It's really good to see you people come to watch football". He looked quite surprised when I shouted back "Don't you patronise me". (John Kerrison)

Within a few months after they had set up home together things started to turn sour between John and Susan. As their relationship worsened they began living separately, he remained downstairs whilst she lived upstairs with her son, and the mortgage became wholly John's liability. The situation deteriorated even further to the point where John sought an eviction order but it took nearly a year for him to gain sole occupancy. Perhaps he had been foolish or expected too much from the relationship. It is possible that, having found his independence, he was searching for a ready made family to replicate his situation prior to the accident. In any event, it all ended badly.

It was a really difficult time... Caroline and Debbie used to come over and meet me in a nearby pub. I was very grateful for their support. (John Kerrison)

About two years later John managed to sell the bungalow and he moved to his current home in Hillingdon; the property came up for sale when the mother of a friend of John's sister passed away. The location, north of the Uxbridge Road and about one and a half miles from Botwell Common Road, was not his first choice but the house had the advantage of being on a corner plot with space to add an extension. There was also a working stairlift already in place and the upstairs bathroom had been adapted for disabled use, this enabled John to live on the upper floor whilst the building work was carried out.

When the ground floor of the property was enlarged and converted for John's use a lot of thought went into the design. This included placing the electric sockets and light switches at a convenient height, comfortably within reach from a wheelchair. The downstairs bathroom was built as a self draining wet room and the kitchen was also customised to accommodate John's wheelchair.

159

When the extension was finished there was ample space to accommodate John's grandfather clock and to display his drum collection.

In 2007 the TV people were looking to hire a wheelchair accessible house to use as a set, they were filming an episode of "New Tricks". I used the money to go on holiday to the West Country. (John Kerrison)

Part V - Searching For a Cure

Chapter Nineteen

*I never did that well with medical people... they made no attempt to correct my spinal-cord... I have a really negative memories about them. Their attitude was "here's your wheelchair, now get on with it". (*John Kerrison)

John has always felt a great deal of bitterness about the lack of any attempt at surgical intervention after the accident and the passing years have failed to diminish his feelings. Despite a six month spirit crushing "incarceration" at Stoke Mandeville Hospital, in the Spinal Injuries Unit, frustratingly nothing was done which might have prevented his paraplegia. He believes that in some ways it would have been better if someone had tried to do something, utilising whatever techniques were available at the time, even if they had failed miserably. Instead John has spent many years wondering if more could have been done or if his current paralysis was an inevitable outcome from his injuries.

A short while after the accident, whilst John was living in self imposed exile in the back room of his parents' house, he was flicking through a popular periodical called "Titbits". He often read such magazines, which his mother brought to him from the outside world, in order to alleviate the boredom of sitting around on his wheelchair. One article in particular caught his eye because it referred to the treatment of patients who had sustained a traumatic spinal injury. He had very little interest in researching any remedial treatments for his own condition but the magazine featured an alternative medical therapy called "acupuncture".

The only guy who really helped me was a Mr Fletcher who was an osteopath and acupuncturist in Southall. It was his attitude of "let's give it a go" that eventually gave me the confidence to start going back out again. (John Kerrison)

The report in Titbits centred on reports from China on the use of acupuncture to treat patients who had incurred paraplegia following spinal injury, the results had apparently been quite encouraging. John found an acupuncture practitioner called Mr Fletcher from the telephone directory whose practise was conveniently situated in nearby Norwood Green Southall. In a "what have I got to lose" moment John gave him a call and explained his circumstances. Mr Fletcher gave him an appointment and, without making John any promises, he offered to see what he could do for him. At twenty-five pounds the consultation fee was by no means cheap but nevertheless John ended up going for treatment twice a week for nearly ten years.

Mr Fletcher was a well built man, possibly from a military background, who had made frequent visits to China in order to increase his knowledge of alternative medicine and to hone his skills; John recalls that he may have actually been the head of the British Acupuncture Association at that time. The acupuncture treatment typically involves the use of thin steel needles, about fifteen centimetres long, which are inserted at an angle into the skin and left in place for twenty minutes or so. Specific points on the body are said to be associated with different medical symptoms. John could feel the pins going into his back but there was no pain, just a quite strange and not unpleasant sensation. Mr Fletcher also employed a variation of the standard acupuncture treatment which is called "moxibustion". The technique also involves a liberal amount of skin pricking but with the addition of heat supplied by burning a cone of special herbs placed on top of the needles.

Perhaps he (Mr Fletcher) was attempting to do the impossible... but he had empathy. He was trying to do something for me, instead of the way that I was treated at Stoke Mandeville. He was the only one

162

who was willing to have a go... perhaps that was the relevance of it.
(John Kerrison)

John got on really well with Mr Fletcher and also with his wife who, as an ex-nurse, contributed to his treatment. There was no immediate and drastic improvement in John's physical health, although over a long period of time he did experience an increase in bladder control. In addition there was a large and uncomfortable lump on John's back which, caused by calcification on his damaged thoracic vertebrae, eventually disappeared a few years after the acupuncture therapy began. These successes were quite small but nevertheless they were significant improvements in the quality of John's life. A much bigger benefit that he experienced from the acupuncture sessions was the dramatic improvement in his mental health. Despite the best efforts of his family and friends John had previously rarely left the self imposed solitude provided by the back room at his parents' house. However, a short while after making contact with Mr Fletcher he was leaving home twice a week to receive treatment. In small increments John began to slowly regain some of his former self-confidence.

What he did wasn't just about the treatment there was also the confidence that he gave me. It gave me, not hope, but something else. It was his caring attitude and the support that he gave me... it was holistic... he treated the whole person and not just the condition.
(John Kerrison)

One day during a therapy session John told Mr Fletcher that his mother was very feeling very poorly. For quite some time Mrs Kerrison had been suffering from shingles, a viral disease which is characterised by an uncomfortable and often extremely painful skin rash; all efforts employing conventional medicine had failed to ease her suffering. Mr Fletcher gave John some homeopathic preparations to take home to his mother, without any charge for his services, and her debilitating shingles were completely gone within four days. Mrs Kerrison was very grateful for his intervention and she never forgot him for it. These days John still relies a great deal on homeopathic remedies including treatment for his hypertension. He has no interest

163

in any scientific doubts about the efficacy of alternative medicine, it's a case of "what works , works" and should be left at that.

An opportunity arose for John to explore a spiritual route to a potential cure when his Roman Catholic friend Malcolm Price invited him to go on a trip to Lourdes. The pilgrimage was organised by a priest called "Father Phil" from the Immaculate Heart of Mary Roman Catholic Church in Hayes. John agreed to go despite his never having had anything much in the way of spiritual faith; he was not religious nor was he a fervent believer in miracles. At the time John was still living in his parents' house and, in view of his demanding behaviour, his absence would provide his mother with a welcome short break. He paid fifty pounds towards the trip even though the church generously offered to fund the entire cost despite knowing that he was neither religious nor a Roman Catholic.

There are a few documented cases of what they call miracles, but if you look at the huge number of people who visit Lourdes every year then the success rate must be about 0.00001%. (John Kerrison)

One of the people travelling to Lourdes was a grandmother called Nelly who had been invited along in the hope that it might relieve her arthritis. John got on well with the older woman who, just the same as him, was only going on the excursion for fun and not for any serious interest in faith healing. The group flew to the Tarbes–Lourdes–Pyrénées Airport and stayed in the Hosanna House residential centre situated less than two miles from Lourdes. The accommodation was run by an order of nuns who were dedicated to looking after disabled visitors. All of the rooms were well equipped with excellent facilities for wheelchair users and the more abled bodied visitors alike. The food was very good and John was also extremely impressed by the fact that alcoholic beverages were available. The atmosphere was quite holiday-like and far from being at all sombre.

Lourdes became an important place of Roman Catholic pilgrimage when, in the mid nineteenth century, an apparition of the Virgin Mary was reputed to have appeared on numerous occasions to Saint Bernadette in the "Grotto of Massabielle". The site later gained a reputation following frequent reports concerning disabled pilgrims who had experienced miraculous healing after bathing in the water from the grotto's well. These days the town of Lourdes has become very commercialised as John discovered for himself when, in order to avoid the interminably long religious services attended by his group, he wandered around the town on his own.

When you are inside the actual place at Lourdes it's quite peaceful and tranquil with religious "Ave Maria" singing and music... but outside it's bustling and full of shops selling souvenir tat like bottles of holy water from Lourdes, holy statues, crosses and everything else under the sun... I half expected to see inflatable nun sex dolls on sale, if you get what I mean. (John Kerrison)

When John visited the grotto he was assisted by the shrine attendants who lowered him into a stone bath filled with water from the sacred well. Unfortunately, when he was lifted out of the water there was no discernible improvement to his condition. There is a very old jest concerning a man who is unable to walk and he decided to make a pilgrimage to Lourdes seeking a miraculous cure. The punch line being that when he came out of the water he found that he was still unable to walk but his wheelchair had been supernaturally bestowed with four new tyres. However, for those who are desperately seeking relief from their ailments, especially when there is no hope left except for divine intervention, it is definitely not a joke.

Strangely the first time that I went to Lourdes I was practically dry when I came out of the water. That really struck me... I didn't go to Lourdes for anything other than the crack... It was actually quite good fun. (John Kerrison)

John must have enjoyed his visit to Lourdes because a few years later, after moving out of his parents' house, he paid to go on a second visit to the holy shrine with a group from the Immaculate Heart of Mary Roman Catholic Church. It wasn't anything to do with religion for John, it was more the fact that he felt included, he was treated as a person and not just someone in a wheelchair. Not all offers of spiritual assistance are quite so welcome and, for some strange reason, being in a wheelchair can sometimes attract the attention of religious zealots.

Some people perceive that they can enter your space and say something to you just because you are sitting in a wheelchair. Recently a woman in Harrow came up to me and she said "Jesus loves you". I told her that she was delusional. Then she asked me "Can I pray for you?" to which I gave her a two word answer. She just said "Thank you" and went away. (John Kerrison)

John had another encounter with a different example of alternative medicine completely by chance when, in the process of renewing his passport, he visited a shop on the Uxbridge Road in Southall Broadway to have the requisite photograph taken. There were automatic photo booths near where he was living in Goshawk Gardens but, in the thoughtless apartheid operated against the disabled, they were impossible to use in a wheelchair. The photography shop proprietor was a Sikh who mentioned that his brother had a degree of paralysis in his legs but, after the affected limbs were massaged with a special oil that was imported from India, he had shown a marked improvement in his mobility.

Motivated by curiosity John decided to experiment and try the mystic Asian treatment for himself. The oil came in a plain glass bottle without any labelling giving details as to its ingredients, origin or instructions for use. Aided by his girlfriend, John rubbed the lotion into his legs everyday for about a month until it ran out. However, apart from the possible benefit to his blood circulation there was no discernible improvement in his condition. It is possible that the oil was a useless "quack" remedy or, because John has no sensation in his legs, perhaps it was not at all appropriate for his particular paraplegic status.

I'm fairly sure… In fact I know… there won't be a complete cure for my condition within my lifetime. (John Kerrison)

Whilst John was an outpatient and volunteer visitor at the Alderbourne Rehabilitation Unit in Hillingdon Hospital he also became a guinea pig for a scientific study involving something called

166

"Functional Electronic Stimulation". He recalls that the experimental project took place in the early 1980s, it was undertaken by a doctor from Wales assisted by an Occupational Therapist and a nurse called Mrs Barrett. Several of the other outpatients and residents took part in the trials including John's friend Trevor Wells who, as a tetraplegic, was unable to move his arms or legs. Trevor had an uncle called Les, he was a retired "boffin" and he became very interested in the electrical experiments.

FES utilises electrical currents to induce activity in the muscles operating the limbs and abdomen, this includes subjects who have experienced paralysis following spinal cord injury. The neurones which control the muscles are electrically active cells and FES exploits this property to produce contractions in the subject's muscle tissue. The principle has been known since the earliest days when electricity was first discovered. School biology lessons commonly demonstrate the effect using dismembered frog legs and the "medicinal use" of electricity has become part of folklore as a result of the tale concerning Dr Frankenstein's monster written by Mary Shelley.

John was wired to the FES equipment with electrodes stuck to his skin, the rubber pads were smeared with a gel and held in place by velcro straps. He felt no sensation whatsoever when different power levels and frequencies of electrical stimulation were employed and the process was only partially successful in getting his paralysed leg muscles to move. It is likely that years of muscle wastage contributed to the limited response that John experienced. However, the reaction from John's leg muscles to FES was significant when compared to the more orthodox patellar reflex response. In the test the ligament below the knee cap is struck with a reflex hammer to produce the classic "knee jerk" involuntary leg kick. In John's case his legs have failed to give any such response since his accident.

The muscle stimulation experiments were carried out at the Rehab Unit in Hillingdon Hospital over a period of around two years with varying degrees of success from patient to patient. When Trevor Wells first experienced the FES it behaved quite unpredictably. Low settings on the machine made his arm muscles twitch but when the electrical power was increased it produced such a violent reaction that it put his shoulder out. He received treatment from an osteopath, a young lady called Shirley. There was another unexpected consequence from the FES experiment when, a few years later in 1990, Trevor and Shirley got married. John was the best man at the wedding.

FES is a much more precise science these days and commercially manufactured machines are available which, designed for home use by able bodied people, are often sold with extravagant claims relating to potential weight loss plus flabby belly reduction. However, the benefits of the treatment for the disabled are far better documented and include better blood circulation with increased muscle mass leading to fewer pressure sores and less frequent violent involuntary spasms. Sequential stimulation of related muscles has given hope to achieving the restoration of functions such as increased bladder and bowel control, hand grasp and perhaps to enable individuals with paraplegia to stand up or even to walk again.

There was a policeman called Phillip Olds who got shot during an armed robbery in Hayes in the mid 1980s; as a result of his injuries he was left paralysed. After leaving hospital he made several attempts to walk again using systems such as FES and his progress often received a great deal of press and television publicity; he also went to the USA to take part in similar mobility experiments. John also tried to walk again at Hillingdon Hospital using leg callipers and the support of parallel bars. It was very similar to the set up that he had used at Stoke Mandeville Spinal Injury Unit but with addition of the experimental FES equipment. However, it was not very successful.

In the end PC Olds committed suicide and I can probably understand why he did it... I've been there and I've got the T-shirt. When you're in a wheelchair the spontaneity has gone from your life and you cannot get your head around everything... he probably wanted to be like he was before it all happened... just like we all do.
(John Kerrison)

Although John sought assistance from the world of alternative medicine such as homeopathy and acupuncture he did not forsake conventional medical treatments. However, he did learn to question and challenge any procedures and prescriptions that he felt were unsuitable, he believes that he knows what is best for his body. A couple of years ago a doctor at Stoke Mandeville Hospital told him that, following a medical procedure, he must take Gentamicin in order to avoid the "certainty" of contracting a bladder infection. John refused to take the powerful antibiotic and, managing the situation himself, he proved the doctor wrong; he had learned from his own past experience.

In the 1980s a surgeon called Mr Gardner informed John about a surgical technique which had the potential to give patients with spinal cord lesion some degree of increased bladder and bowel control. The "Brindley implant", otherwise known as the "sacral root stimulator", involves placing an electronic device in the back next to the spine. The implant is then operated by an external transmitter, or sometimes just a simple magnet, in order to stimulate the appropriate neural pathways which have been isolated by damage to the spinal cord. The surgeon was quite willing to undertake the operation but John turned down his offer when he was informed that the success rate was only about one in four at that time. Nevertheless, for many people who have incurred a spinal injury the benefits of being fitted with an implant outweigh all of the inherent risks and disadvantages of the surgical intervention.

Recent developments concerning the use of stem cell implants have been very encouraging. Whilst many of the reports centre on the possibility of paralysed legs walking once again it is much more likely that in many cases stem cell therapy will produce comparatively modest results. However, even minor improvements in muscle control could be of enormous benefit for paraplegic and tetraplegic patients. It has been a long time coming, John recalls reading a newspaper article in 1976 which promised just such a scientific breakthrough in the treatment of spinal injury.

Part VI - Mobility

Chapter Twenty

A lot of disabled people rely on having a car to be independent...
to go to work, to go shopping, to attend hospital treatment, to
socialise, and so on... Successive governments keep on attacking
mobility benefits whilst at the same time they fail to make public
transport more accessible. (John Kerrison)

Despite the best efforts of the Spinal Injuries Unit at Stoke
Mandeville Hospital to make John "normal" he failed to master
walking in the tailor made leg callipers which they supplied to him.
When he was discharged from the hospital in 1971 he was issued
with a wheelchair made by a company called Everest and Jennings
and a telephone number to call if anything mechanical went wrong.
John bitterly recalls the lack of empathy shown towards him and the
ethos being very much along the lines of "there's your chair, now get
on with it". Wheelchairs at that time were characteristically very
robust but they were also heavy and unmanageable, even those which
were capable of being folded and carried in the boot of a car were
quite cumbersome. There was also a very limited "one size fits all"
range of wheelchairs available which often made them
uncomfortable and, when used for long periods of time, had the
potential to cause pressure sores.

   In the late 1980s John gave a talk to the American Women's
Association in Ruislip about the challenges that he faced as a result
of his disability. They gave him a monetary grant of about twelve
hundred pounds which enabled him to buy a lightweight folding

wheelchair. The high tech design greatly assisted him in his day-to-day life, especially when going through the tricky manoeuvre of transferring from his wheelchair to his car. Through years of practise John has developed a high degree of athleticism when completing such transfers, a task which he much prefers to do unaided, utilising the strong shoulder muscles that he has developed since losing the use of his legs.

The situation regarding wheelchairs has seen great improvements since the days when John first became disabled. The NHS currently operates a voucher system and wheelchairs are now available which are tailor made on an individual basis. Currently John's own bespoke chair cost around three thousand pounds and is predominantly constructed from titanium alloy, a metal which produces a strong but lightweight structure. In addition the well fitting seat and a "Jay" cushion allow him to sit in the wheelchair for long periods without causing any problems concerning pressure sores. The wheels cost more than a hundred pounds each and are fitted with "Kevlar" reinforced puncture proof tyres, solid rubber tyres have been largely replaced by pneumatic versions which give a much more comfortable ride over bumpy surfaces. The NHS voucher system gives a choice between two lease service contracts under which the wheelchair is normally replaced every five years.

There are no handles or brake levers on the back of John's custom built wheelchair, he prefers to propel himself rather than being assisted by a "helper" except when going uphill. He shows an incredible sense of balance when leaning his chair backwards to mount a high pavement kerb and he is rarely foiled when a step or two might prevent him entering a pub. Manual wheelchairs have several benefits compared to their battery powered counterparts, they provide good exercise and enable greater accessibility.

World War II left many ex-servicemen disabled and an iconic three wheeled car was designed specifically to give them mobility. The "Invacar" was manufactured with a motorcycle engine and a fibreglass shell which was usually a distinctive ice blue colour; inside there was only room for the driver and a stowed wheelchair. The invalid carriages were all owned by the government and supplied to disabled people on a lease through a system administered by the Department of Health and Social Security. When the DHSS offered to supply John with his own Invacar he turned it down.

The compact vehicles were often ridiculed as "Noddy cars" and had a well earned reputation for being dangerously unstable deathtraps. Formula One world champion racing driver Graham Hill famously refused to drive one and he campaigned for them to be replaced by a less dangerous alternative. European Union regulations eventually proved to be far too stringent for the Invacar and sounded the death knell for the little car. In 2003 the government recalled and scrapped its entire stock of the vehicles. Currently the DWP operates a scheme funded by the Mobility component of the claimant's DLA "Disability Living Allowance". Those who qualify can lease a car with the running costs including vehicle excise duty, insurance, servicing, tyres and breakdown cover, paid by monthly instalments.

John started driving again about four or five years after the accident and has owned a number of vehicles which, to avoid the need for foot pedal controls, have all had automatic gearboxes. Starting with a Hillman Avenger he then went for a brown Ford Cortina followed by a silver Ford Cortina estate. He then owned two Nissan Prairies in a row before changing to his current vehicle which is a Kia Sedona. Hand controls have improved a great deal in recent years and John is particularly impressed by the current conversion kits which are easy to use, plus they are quite simple to fit or remove when required.

In the past car insurance was typically expensive for disabled drivers. Often the premiums were "loaded" because the disabled were erroneously assessed as presenting a higher risk. Fortunately that is no longer the case and motor insurance is now offered at a much more equitable cost. Also the stickers proclaiming "Disabled Driver - No Hand Signals" on the rear of a vehicle have become rather obsolete. Nowadays almost all drivers rely completely on using the indicator switch rather than waving their right arm out of the side window, except when performing gestures not actually illustrated in the Highway Code.

The Eurotunnel Shuttle provides an opportunity to travel under the English Channel and visit Calais in order to purchase cut price wines and beers. John has gone shopping in France several times using the service and, whilst travelling in his own vehicle inside the

Shuttle, he has often wondered how they would evacuate disabled passengers in the event of an emergency; there is not enough room on either side to fully open the car door. John and one of his friends also used the Shuttle on a trip to deliver a new wheelchair to Trevor Wells who was living in Minorca. They shared the driving all the way down to Barcelona where they caught the ferry to the Balearic Islands.

Italy has always occupied a special place in John's heart ever since he went there as a teenager in the 1960s as a member of The Eccentrics. Many years later he travelled to Italy with two former members of The Bad Boys; the Northolt band had taken over the resident spot at the Piper Club after The Eccentrics had finished their contract. They flew out to Milan and then took the scenic train ride down to Rome. The Piper Club was still operating, but they didn't go in because of the difficulty in getting John down the steep staircases. Instead they spent quite some time hanging around outside and reminiscing about the old days.

In 1997 he flew out direct to Rome, this time travelling on his own, and he was picked up at the airport by Mick Liddell. The former lead singer in The Eccentrics had been deported from the country but returned later travelling on a passport using the surname taken by his mother when she remarried. He was running a business restoring cars and exporting them back and forth from Sweden to Italy. Mick took John to the Piper Club and arranged for him to be carried inside down the stairs. The venue was hosting a party to celebrate the fiftieth birthday of the famous Italian singer and songwriter called Frederico Troiani. It was a nostalgic evening but everything had changed inside the club since John and Mick had played there in the 1960s.

John has also travelled to Sicily twice. On the first visit he went with a friend whose sister's wedding was being held on the Mediterranean isle. In the late 1990s John was receiving treatment in hospital and he met a Sicilian man called Salvatore Rosselli who had been injured in an accident. They kept in touch afterwards and Salvatore invited John to come and stay at his home in Casteldaccia near Palermo where he lived with his wife and child, plus his parents and other relatives, in a complex built on top of his shirt factory. John went there for two weeks and had a wonderful time, taking the opportunity to practise speaking Italian. Salvatore was quite wealthy, he and his family were excellent hosts and would not let John spend any of his own money during the time that he stayed with them.

I flew to Magaluf in the late 1990s, there was about a dozen of us. One of my mates got a packet of Marlboro cigarettes and emptied them all out to fill them with dope. We all went to a party and got stoned out of our heads. I also flew to Torremolinos a couple of times with my friend Trevor Wells. Then I went to Tenerife with another mate of mine, I especially remember eating the lovely new potatoes grown on the volcanic soil. (John Kerrison)

A well planned trip to Canada nearly fell apart when unforeseen circumstances forced John's travelling companion to pull out just forty-eight hours before they were due to depart. Whilst John's Asian friend was good enough to stump up the four hundred pounds cost of the flight ticket it still left him without anyone to travel with. In desperation John went around the EMI Social Club in Hayes asking if there was anyone with a passport who wanted to go to Canada and was able to travel at such short notice. A man called Clive Avery said that he would like to go if he could get time off from work.

I didn't really know Clive Avery very well at that time... he told me that I knew his gran, she was Nelly who I went to Lourdes with... I soon became very good friends with Clive. (John Kerrison)

All of this took place on a Thursday and they were due to fly out on the following Saturday; fortunately Clive's employer granted his request for leave. The pair flew to Toronto and booked into their hotel. When John suggested that they should hire a car Clive looked out of the hotel window and was horrified to see the busy freeway with six lanes of traffic going each way. He was a little bit concerned about the prospect of driving in the unfamiliar city, especially as he had only recently passed his driving test.

I met two ladies in the hotel bar and we had a lot to drink. One of them said she would come back and see me after she had taken her friend home. I was completely drunk and I went to bed... later I got a phone call from the receptionist who said that there was a woman at the desk, but he wouldn't let her go up to my room. I had to work hard in order to convince him that she wasn't a prostitute. (John Kerrison)

Clive hired a "rent a wreck" car and they drove to a town in Ontario called Newmarket which is situated about two hours north of Toronto. A friend of Clive's lived there and they stayed at her mother's house. It was very much a "Country & Western" area and one evening they all went to an open-air gig. John overindulged drinking and smoking dope and Clive had to drive him home. After putting John to bed Clive went all the way back to the gig and didn't come back until morning.

Shortly after they had returned to Toronto Clive began to experience a diabetic "hypo" event when he took one of his three daily insulin injections in anticipation of having a substantial meal. They had gone out to eat but then discovered that the restaurant was closed.

Back at the hotel Clive ordered a sandwich from room service and I told him that it wasn't enough. I said "You're not thinking straight because you're having a hypo, you need more to eat than that". He said "It's OK, I've already ordered a hamburger and chips as well". (John Kerrison)

John's cousin Kenny Rogers worked for Air Canada and, accompanied by his daughter, he flew in from London. They all met up and together they drove a hire car all the way down from Toronto to Niagara. John was feeling very tired after the long journey and he went to bed early.

The motel bed in Niagara was one of those vibrating things. Clive and the others put a load of money in the box at the end of the bed and they switched on the vibrations. Then they took my wheelchair away and left me there while they went out for the evening.... I couldn't switch it off and I couldn't escape. (John Kerrison)

From Niagara they drove to New York, it was a long way so Clive and Kenny took turns driving. Unfortunately on the way back to Toronto from NewYork Kenny got a ticket for speeding on the freeway, travelling in excess of the strictly enforced 50 mph limit. The group caught the train down to Montreal where Kenny and his daughter took a flight back to London. John had a cousin living in Montreal who he called "Aunty June", he and Clive stayed at her house for about a week before flying home.

I went to a music shop to try and buy some special drum sticks which are made of bundles of plastic "multi rods", they are quite hard to describe. I discovered that they speak mostly French in Montreal... When I tried to explain what I wanted it all got very comical. (John Kerrison)

The following year John went to the USA accompanied by Clive Avery who brought along his wife plus somebody else from the pub. They flew to New York and stayed for a while with a friend who had emigrated to New Jersey. They then set off in a hire car down the US east coast to Miami, along the Atlantic seaboard, with John acting as the group's navigator. Clive drove the whole way because their travelling companion claimed to have left his driving licence at home. John suspects that the forgotten licence story was fabricated through fear of the daunting traffic system.

Chris Jackson persuaded John to fly to the US one year, the former rhythm guitarist in The Casuals was working for an airline company and promised him a heavily discounted return ticket for the normally expensive flight. John was slightly apprehensive because the journey would involve travelling on his own and meeting up with Chris later. He flew out to Los Angeles and hired a car fitted with hand controls without any major problems. However, he had some difficulty getting used to the American throttle and brake controls which, instead of the more usual push and pull operation, work in an arc motion.

I had known Chris since I was sixteen. He was short and fat whereas I was always thin and gangly... he was a really great guy. We went to Monterey north of LA because his cousin lived up there...

176

I drove him in my hire car and we up through Carmel and past Salinas California where James Dean crashed his car and died in 1955. (John Kerrison)

The trip to the USA was not all about sightseeing, it was also a business trip. Chris had a small music shop in Hanwell called "Monterey Music" which specialised in selling vintage guitars and amplifiers. Whilst he was in California he went to as many swap meets, charity shops and pawn shops as possible, buying up stock to sell and sending it back to England as freight with the airline that he worked for. The timing of the visit was set to coincide with the "NAMM", the North American Music Merchants trade show, which has been held in Anaheim every January since 1901. Chris and John stayed in a Japanese motel called "Kona Kai" situated conveniently near the convention centre hosting the NAMM event.

The motel room only had a bath, there was no disability shower. Chris had a bath and then he asked me if I wanted one, he lifted me in okay but when it came to lifting me out it was a farce. We were both naked and we were falling about the place... we couldn't stop laughing...it would have looked very odd. (John Kerrison)

The NAMM trade show was a huge event with a large number of stalls and every major company in the music business had representatives in attendance selling their wares. Chris seemed to know just about everybody and he introduced John to a lot of interesting people. This included a man called James Burton who was Elvis Presley's guitarist, a nephew of Eddie Cochran and Seymour Duncan (who made guitar pickups for many of the top Rock guitarists) plus several other famous musicians. Subsequently John flew to LA to go to the NAMM trade show for about four years in a row. In 1994 he went accompanied by drummer Steve Holland and they experienced a major earthquake which, centred in the San Fernando Valley, resulted in more than fifty fatalities plus some very costly damage to the buildings and the infrastructures.

Chris couldn't get used to the American way of greeting people... they can sometimes sound a little bit false. We went to a store in

Fullerton where they were having a sale, Chris really liked a bargain. A shop assistant said "How are you doing today Sir?" and then, further on, another guy asked "And how's your day Sir?"... Chris turned to him and said "What the xxxx's it got to do with you?" (John Kerrison)

In 2010 John travelled to Australia with his eldest sister. En route they stopped off for four days in Singapore where they visited the famous Raffles bar; they followed tradition by drinking Singapore Slings and throwing their peanut shells on the floor. When they arrived in Perth Annette stayed with Janette, a former neighbour from Botwell Common Road who had moved from Hayes to North Perth. John stayed with Frankie Reid, the former front man for The Casuals who was living in the south of the city.

Australia is a lot like the USA in that there are loads of new buildings... everything is built under regulations which demand good wheelchair access. (John Kerrison)

When John discovered that Deep Purple were booked to play at the Perth HBF Stadium on 5 May 2010 he sent an e-mail to his old friend Ian Gillan and was rewarded with four back stage passes for the concert.

Wheelchair access in the stadium was really good, we were allowed to watch the band from quite close to the stage. Me and Frankie Reid overindulged on the large Jack Daniels served from the hospitality bar. After the show Ian Gillan introduced me to his friend Dennis Lillie the famous Australian cricketer. (John Kerrison)

After four weeks in Perth John and his sister travelled to Brisbane and stayed for a week with one of their cousins who had settled there. John took the opportunity to spend a few days with his friend Jimmy Royal who was living in a place called Toowoomba situated about an hour and a half drive from Brisbane. John had played several times with the James Royal Set on BBC radio. When John and Annette travelled back to the UK they stopped over at Hong Kong for a few days.

Travelling by air has improved a great deal for wheelchair users since the early days...they didn't use to let you travel alone, you had to have a "carer" with you... there is a much improved attitude these days, the airlines are more disability aware... It varies around the world, the USA is the best because they have better transfer chairs and more training. Australia is a close second and Britain is very poor; Heathrow is easily the worst in my opinion. (John Kerrison)

John later paid a second visit to Australia, stopping off for one night at Kuala Lumpur. He was accompanied by his friend Reg Bodman who he has known since the 1960s when, as teenage scooter driving Mods, they played together in Frankie Reid and the Casuals. It was something of a band reunion when they met up with Frankie Reid himself. On the way home John and Reg stopped off at Kuala Lumpur for four days. Unfortunately the hotel failed to honour their promise of a bedroom converted for disabled use, there were no transfer rails in the bathroom and John had to rely on assistance from Reg.

Part VII - Protest

(It should be noted that the opinions expressed below are not
necessarily those held by DASH - the Disablement Association of
Hillingdon - or its constituent membership)

Chapter Twenty - One

*One in seven of the population has a disability but they have a
very small voice... most of them have paid Income Tax and National
Insurance all of their lives. Many disabled people are too quiet and
always grateful for what should be theirs as a right and not
stigmatised as charity. I'm different... I've got a very big gob.* (John
Kerrison)

Ann Powell was not just John's social worker, in the years after
being assigned as his case officer she also became his friend and
confidante; to some extent they both ended up counselling each other
about their problems. Her straight talking manner, direct if not blunt,
was a trait which John had always appreciated and she played an
important role in aiding his rehabilitation after the accident; a
painfully slow process which took nearly a decade for him find some
level of self worth and independence. It was under Ann's advice that
John should "get off his backside and do something constructive"
that he became a volunteer helper at the Alderbourne Long Stay
Disabled Unit at Hillingdon Hospital.

Subsequently Ann suggested that John should get more involved
with helping other disabled people; she told him about a local
organisation called DASH, the "Disablement Association of
Hillingdon". John had never actively sought the company of disabled

people, both before and after his accident, but nevertheless in 1986 he started going to the DASH meetings. Since then he has been an active member, campaigning on issues concerning disability, for twenty-eight years. He has held various important positions in DASH including that of access advice officer, disability awareness lecturer, spokesperson and chairperson.

I have friends who are disabled but our friendship has little to do with disability... I have two very good friends, Trevor Wells and Marilyn Loosely, but we would have been good friends even if we had met in entirely different circumstances outside of the world of disability. (John Kerrison)

DASH was originally formed in 1984 and at first it ran on a shoestring budget based at St John's Hospital, Kingston Lane in Uxbridge until the building was demolished; the site was later developed as an extension to Brunel University. Currently DASH operates from offices at Wood End Green Road in Hayes and its aim is to provide a support structure for disabled people in the borough, to assist their carers, to aid their families, and to challenge the negative perceptions concerning disability which are inherent in society. Their mission statement is succinctly summarised as "Disability does not mean inability". When John joined DASH he was introduced to a lady called Marilyn Loosely who was a founder member and the association's director. As a fellow wheelchair user, born with spina bifida, she helped him to get involved and also to feel included.

John had always found it difficult to mix with disabled people, even after the accident he still didn't feel that he was one of "them". During his enforced "incarceration" in the Spinal Injuries Unit at Stoke Mandeville Hospital and as an outpatient at Hillingdon Hospital John had met many other disabled people. He had found several of them to be very demanding and extremely insular, refusing to join society and at the same time complaining about exclusion. It was a condition which John understood well from his own experience of hiding away in the seclusion of the back room at his parents' house and his own extremely demanding behaviour towards his mother in particular.

I was really surprised when Marylyn Loosely pointed out to me that there was a strange form of snobbery amongst some people with spinal injuries... a few of them consider themselves to be in the "higher class" of disabled people, which made me laugh. Marylyn referred to them as the "Super crips". (John Kerrison)

One of John's concerns about joining an organisation like DASH was that he would meet a group of disabled people who were totally obsessed with "political correctness". He believes that the penalties for using non PC words are sometimes more severe than for really important examples of discrimination. John feels that this can lead to a situation whereby actions which have huge repercussions on the quality of life experienced by people who have a disability go largely unnoticed; deeds having far greater consequences than words. However, he does tell people that he is no more "confined to a wheelchair" than they are confined to their shoes, he much prefers the expression "wheelchair user" but doesn't really mind what nomenclature is actually used.

There are much more important issues than all the PC stuff about words... it's just part of the lip service. How can you go to work if you can't get up the stairs or if they don't have the right toilet facilities? (John Kerrison)

Much of the prejudice which contributes to the exclusion of disabled people from society stems from a mixture of guilt, ignorance, fear and lack of empathy. Prior to his accident John himself held just such negative opinions towards the disabled. As a child growing up in Hayes he had been frightened by the charity collection box, modelled to resemble a "spastic" boy wearing leg callipers, which stood outside a local shop. John admits that he would cross the road to avoid the life sized mannequin or if he saw someone in a wheelchair. Furthermore, he and his friends often used discriminatory language concerning the disabled. All of this, together with his straight talking loudmouth, made him an ideal candidate to represent DASH as a disability awareness officer.

When John gave half day seminars on the subject of disability awareness he was often accompanied by a colleague called Simon Harris, a very laid back character who had total visual impairment; a condition which John refers to, in his non PC parlance, as being "blind". The disability training courses included activities such as everyone writing down all of the negative words that they can think of associated with disability and then the positive words, provoking group discussion concerning the presumptions and assumptions commonly held about disabled people. Practical exercises using blindfolds, sight obscuring glasses and wheelchairs give a greater understanding of the barriers faced by the disabled. The participants are encouraged to have fun, despite the serious objectives concerning disability awareness, and the seminars are also an excellent format for use as a team building exercise. DASH is ideally placed to give advice concerning the implications and statutory requirements of the Disability Discrimination Act.

The Disability Discrimination Act was a piece of legislation which was constructed without any understanding whatsoever of the main disability issues... it often seems to me that all it does is help the lawyers to make more money. (John Kerrison)

Sometimes campaigning for disability rights can prove to be a very uphill battle, even in areas where the best of intentions prevail. One year DASH booked the Hayes Working Men's club as the venue for their annual general meeting. However, attendance at the AGM was rather restricted because under Health & Safety regulations they were only allowed to have two wheelchair users present. The mandatory licences issued for a building's use often carry such restrictions, wheelchairs are regarded as an obstructive danger to safe evacuation in the event of a serious fire or other major emergencies.

DASH organised a training session for the staff at Heathrow who are responsible for transferring disabled passengers on and off the airplanes. We told them that the way that they did things was not very good and we offered advice on how to improve the way that they treated people. They insisted they were doing the right thing and they would not listen to us at all. (John Kerrison)

183

On another occasion John and his colleagues at DASH were asked to set up a disability seminar for MPs. The intention was to supply the parliamentary politicians with wheelchairs so that they could experience for themselves the access and mobility issues faced by the disabled, but the seminar failed to materialise due to a lack of interest amongst those booked to take part. Democratically elected officials from the world of politics rarely find time for anything that isn't a "vote winner" with the general public. It is a rather short sighted view because disability affects not just each individual disabled person but also everyone around them. There is often a major impact on the lives of partners, family and friends of people who become mentally or physically disabled.

There are people who talk a lot of rhetoric but haven't got a clue... especially the politicians. I met the Home Secretary once... We were trying to sort out some things about disabled access in Hayes town... It was frustrating because it wasn't worth talking to him. (John Kerrison)

John's background in the construction industry was put to good use when he was appointed as the access officer for DASH. As part of his duties he attended weekly meetings at the Civic Centre, sitting with the architects and the town planners in the council, discussing the designs which had been proposed for new public buildings. People are living longer and therefore there will be more disabled people in the future. Despite such obvious demographics many new construction projects often have poor access and little scope for any later adaptations. To John every single small detail was important and he made sure that the council complied with all the regulations regarding access for the disabled.

In the event of fire drills and real emergencies the lifts are usually put out of operation. Wheelchair users have to be manhandled down the stairs in special "evacuation chairs"... it is a horrible experience. New buildings should be constructed with lifts which are still safe to use in the event of fire, they should be concrete lined and have an independent power source. (John Kerrison)

Sometimes the architects and planners may have thought that John was being a bit on the tough side because he rarely compromises on anything that he passionately believes in. He was able to identify access problems from his own experience as a wheelchair user and, using the practical knowledge that he had gained from working in the construction industry, he could also often offer a solution. The council invited him to apply for a permanent post as a full time access officer for the borough but, despite the financial inducement of a salaried position and other benefits, he turned them down.

I didn't apply for the council job as an access officer because I thought that I could do more on the outside... if I was a public servant I couldn't open my mouth on every subject. I didn't want to be part of the establishment...I didn't want to join them... Often they just look for a "yes man" and I don't follow sheep. (John Kerrison)

DASH is not just in the business of giving enlightening talks on the subject of disability rights to planners, politicians, employers and the general public. When the need arises the DASH membership is quite ready to take much more direct action and John has helped to organise more than one such militant protest. In the early 1990s the London Underground Station at Hillingdon was demolished as part of a new road traffic scheme which required the rerouting of the A40 Western Avenue. The station was rebuilt and opened in December 1992 without any consultation with disabled groups such as DASH.

As a result the design gave little thought to the repercussions for disabled passengers and included steps at the station entrance. Wheelchair users wishing to travel westwards, in the direction of Uxbridge, were forced to go up a ramp from the car park and then summon assistance by ringing a bell. If station staff were available they would respond by operating the lift. In addition there was a wheelchair challenging step up from the Metropolitan line platforms into the carriages and an equally perilous step down in order to enter the Piccadilly line carriages.

The "powers that be" failed to see any element of discrimination in the set up which often kept disabled passengers waiting for long periods of time or, as often as not, left them stranded and completely excluded from the public transport system. One day John and his fellow protesters from DASH and elsewhere occupied the station during the morning rush hour; they stopped the trains running for five or six hours causing chaos. Some of the activists actually got onto the tracks whilst a few others chained themselves to the bogeys. They called it "the train spotters' charter" because disabled passengers could get onto the station platforms and see the trains but they were unable to get on board.

A large number of commuters were inconvenienced and they complained when they found that they could not get into London. The DASH members answered them by saying that they also wanted to get to London and that's why they were protesting, it was because of the lack of disabled access. John was selected by DASH to be their spokesperson and explain the reason behind the disruptive protest in an interview on a BBC radio news programme. He told them that the situation was unfair and discriminatory, all stations should be built to a design which enabled disabled passengers to travel instead of excluding them from using public transport.

Access on the Eurostar passenger trains is just like so many other stations... if the platforms were level with the carriages then they would not need to put a ramp down for wheelchairs. (John Kerrison)

In 1994 Hillingdon Station was awarded the little known accolade of "London Underground Station of the Year" despite the complaints concerning disabled access; perhaps demonstrating an astonishing lack of concern for wheelchair passengers. John believes that only a small proportion of the nearly three hundred stations in the London Underground system have step free access, somewhere between ten to twenty percent. It is a rather subjective assessment because it depends on what is regarded as step free; barely more than a dozen stations have platforms which provide complete level entry as the vast majority require a step up or down into the train carriage. Despite political promises and pledges the situation has barely improved over the past two or three decades. Some mainline railway stations require twenty-four hours notice from wheelchair passengers; often only one member of a pairs of disabled travellers is allowed to board a train and their companion is placed in a taxi.

The other day I went to a Deep Purple concert in London and I was lucky enough to be able to travel to it on public transport... but there was still a drop of more than 15 cm onto the platform when I got off the Underground train. (John Kerrison)

Some years ago a disability rights group chained themselves to a London Transport bus in a protest concerning the manifold deficiencies in disabled access to transport. Several people were arrested by the police but, with an incredible twist of irony, all the charges had to be dropped because of the insurmountable barrier to justice provided by the steep steps leading up to the magistrates court. The lack of wheelchair access excluded the protesters from the legal process in addition to the transport system, you really couldn't make it up. More recently there has been a relatively wide scale introduction of "kneeling" buses and also buses fitted with hydraulic ramps, both of which facilitate the entry of wheelchairs and mobility scooters.

The situation is still far from being perfect. John has personally experienced several incidents where the space inside the bus set aside for wheelchair users to travel in safety was blocked with shopping, suitcases or kids in buggies; the latter and most common example contravenes the instructions that push chairs should be folded and placed out of the way, it also breaches the provisions of the 2010 Equality Act. John is usually very quick to loudly vocalise his opinion on the matter with those whose thoughtlessness and downright bad manners make much of the provisions for disabled passengers completely redundant.

I went up to London with DASH to give a talk to the Ministry of Transport... the government guys seemed really interested in what we had to say about disabled access... it was very encouraging. (John Kerrison)

Another misuse of the facilities for the disabled that irks John is that concerning disabled parking. At face value the scheme appears to be a valuable benefit for the disabled. However, poor enforcement in cases of misuse of the parking places and the issue of disabled parking permits to people who are not physically disabled devalues the entire system. A similar situation appears to be the case for a scheme designed to provide transport by taxi for the disabled. John and other DASH members have made frequent complaints concerning incidents where they have booked a cab but it failed to turn up; the suspicion being that the taxi drivers may be answering calls which provide a more lucrative income, a discriminatory "I'm not going south of the river at this time of night" situation. There are also reports of instances where taxicab drivers have refused to take passengers who are accompanied by guide dogs.

Chapter Twenty - Two

*The government just fobs off the disabled with piecemeal stuff...
they don't make any real effort. Accessible transport, accessible
work places and accessible shops... it should all be accessible and
usable for all... that's the bottom line for me.* (John Kerrison)

Despite the valuable collective purchasing power of disabled
consumers many businesses make no attempt to attract their custom.
Two-thirds of British holiday resorts lack even basic facilities for
disabled people, a situation which has never really been addressed
even though disabled people want to go on holiday just like anyone
else. When John's friend Trevor and his wife Shirley visit him they
stay in accommodation that is supposed to welcome disabled people.
However, they found that all of the area outside the hotel was
covered in loose gravel, a near impossible surface to cope with in an
electric wheelchair; the cost of resurfacing with tarmac or concrete is
said to be too expensive.

*It's always done piecemeal... disability is always the "poor
relation", always the last in line when it comes to money. The usual
attitude is "they don't mind" and "they'll manage somehow".* (John
Kerrison)

The "we know what's best for you" attitude is unfortunately quite
common amongst those who hold the reins of government. When the
new Hayes bypass was under construction the powers that be agreed
that a pedestrian crossing, at the intersection with the Uxbridge
Road, should be in the form of a bridge spanning the carriageway
high above the traffic. Without any consultation it was decided that
this represented the most suitable option for everyone, including the
disabled. No understanding was shown concerning the potentially

difficult gradient for wheelchair users or the fear experienced from being in such vulnerably high isolation. John and his colleagues at DASH successfully campaigned for a ground level crossing.

Most of the bigger chain stores on the high street cater for disability and wheelchairs because disabled people have spending power. However, many shops don't even have a ramp entrance to allow wheelchair access. John gets very annoyed when the shelf fillers thoughtlessly fill a shop's aisles with produce and don't leave enough space for a wheelchair to pass through. If he finds that his route is blocked he has been known to knock over or to throw the offending items out of his way; the shop workers often react as if he is mentally retarded even when he attempts to explain his rebellious behaviour. When John travelled to the USA he found that they have minimum enforced distances to provide disabled access in shops and premises which are open to the public. European Union regulations detail circumstances where disabled access should be provided at no extra cost but in the United Kingdom, where slavish adherence to EU directives appears to be the norm, such rulings concerning disability are rarely enforced. Even the ancient Colosseum in Rome has now achieved near total wheelchair accessibility.

Recently I went to have a look around the Kew Palace at Kew Gardens... it's a Grade 1 listed building and yet it's still accessible in a wheelchair. When it was restored, a few years back, they added an external lift shaft to the west-wing for disabled access... anything is possible if there is a will to get it done. (John Kerrison)

The emphasis placed upon sporting activities at Stoke Mandeville Hospital, as part of their programme to rehabilitate spinal injury patients, initiated the modern day Paralympics. In 2005 the United Kingdom made a successful bid to host the 2012 Olympic Games and the parallel international competition for disabled athletes. At that time bold promises were made that it would be the most accessible Olympic Games ever held in the history of the four yearly event. Afterwards the London Olympics and Paralympics were judged to have been a spectacular success despite the huge amount of tax payers' money required to subsidise the cost of the massive enterprise. Television coverage was quite excellent, which is just as well because little of that money went towards increasing disabled access to public transport and the well publicised pledges typically remain broken.

We are not all athletes... the majority of able-bodied people don't do such things so why should everyone think that disabled people would do it... I went out shopping and someone shouted "What are you going to do in the Paralympics?"... I gave him a suitable response. (John Kerrison)

John is less than enthusiastic about sporting events for the disabled and, whilst recognising the courage and determination of the participants, he would much prefer to watch football. He would like to see an equally large "Olympic" effort and expenditure made towards items such as accessibility, something which would benefit the greater population of people with disabilities. Sporting activities which increase awareness concerning disability are a positive move but they fail to portray ordinary people and the day-to-day barriers that they face. In some ways such events can tend to give a false illusion of equality, especially when "spun" for political gain.

Without equality what are we?... I know that total equality can never fully exist but there should be at least some decent attempt to strive for that level of inclusion. (John Kerrison)

There are around seven million disabled people of working age in the United Kingdom and about half of them are unemployed. The government organisation REMPLOY was set up around seventy years ago to provide employment for ex-servicemen and others with severe disabilities. Several factories were opened around the UK giving jobs to the many disabled people who would otherwise find it extremely difficult to obtain work. These facilities were heavily subsidised from the public purse and in recent times they were closed on the grounds of fiscal prudence; it was argued that the money could be better spent elsewhere. Subsequently more than half of the REMPLOY workers failed to find alternative employment and, in the absence of a paid salary, they were presumably left entirely dependent on State benefits; an extra expense which surely must have diminished the amount of any money saved.

It was totally shortsighted... those people lost their work, their social contact, their self-respect and their independence... all of those social issues were completely ignored... they were left with no future. (John Kerrison)

The ethos behind the National Insurance Act of 1946 centred around a guiding principle that benefits and medical treatment should be dispensed as a right and devoid of all stigma. By virtue of having paid National Insurance John qualified for Industrial Injuries Benefits in respect of the injuries that he incurred at work. He had no problems with the benefits system except for a rather bizarre annual medical examination to ensure that he had not undergone a miraculous recovery.

However, these days the disabled have to undergo rigorous medical assessments, put out to tender from private health companies, in an inequitable regime which many believe has more to do with political vote catching than fraud detection. Huge delays in the payment of disability benefits are an inevitable consequence of such disproportionate policies. Other hardships have been imposed upon the disabled community including the so called "bedroom tax" and the cuts in Social Services. Charities have been left to fill the gaps in a backward step, reinforcing a "handouts" stigma to the benefits system.

Millionaire politicians claim to understand disability because they have a disabled relative or dependant... they should try living in the real world with the massive budget cuts that they've made... It was that sort of thing that made me think of joining DASH... I wanted to feel integrated and I wanted to have my four pennyworth. (John Kerrison)

John is very critical of the treatment that he received whilst he was a patient at the Spinal Injuries Unit in Stoke Mandeville Hospital. If anyone wishes to challenge his negative assessment of the wold renowned institution then they should consider that Stoke

Mandeville, along with several other NHS hospitals, were very busy falling over themselves to accommodate the disc jockey Jimmy Saville. Their sycophantic obsession with the famous radio and television star increased over the years as he accumulated astonishing sums of money in charitable donations, amounting to several million pounds, which eventually helped fund the building of a new Spinal Injuries Unit and several other projects. In the face of increasing allegations and rumours concerning Saville's behaviour a few organisations distanced themselves from him, whilst Stoke Mandeville and several others took a blinkered or even a decidedly blindfolded approach.

It gave Jimmy Saville the whip hand because if they exposed him he could pull the money out... reliance on charity produces monsters like Saville... NHS treatment should be paid for by the State as a right and not as a charity handout. (John Kerrison)

It is now apparent that Jimmy Saville was a self serving predatory sexual pervert and the statistical list of his victims grows as the belated investigation into his behaviour proceeds. John believes that many more people were indirectly harmed by Saville in addition to those that he molested. The founding principle of the National Health Service was that it should provide free medical treatment funded by general taxation and National Insurance contributions. In addition to the numerous crimes that Saville perpetrated on vulnerable individuals he also made it acceptable that NHS treatment should be subject to a degree of charitable largesse rather than as a basic human right.

There are tons of drummer jokes in the music business... A drummer goes into a shop and asks to buy a guitar. The man behind the counter says "You must be a drummer". The drummer asks him how he knew and he replies "Because this is a wet fish shop"... Then they say "What's the definition of a drummer?... it's a guy who hangs out with musicians". (John Kerrison)

Whilst the jokes about "stupid" Rock drummers is a fairly recent phenomenon, the somewhat similar concept linking disability with

193

low intelligence has been around much longer. The discriminatory misconception can probably be traced back in part to the Victorian era, many of those who exhibited mental or physical impairment were consigned to the "care" of austere workhouses and mental hospitals. Put out of sight, hidden away where no one saw them, they became institutionalised; such lack of integration contributes to present day discrimination. However, nobody really doubts the intellectual capabilities of Professor Stephen Hawking. An iconic figure in his electric wheelchair, the internationally famous theoretical physicist is almost entirely paralysed and he is only able to "speak" by virtue of an electronic voice synthesiser; a sound generator which operates in a similar way to John's drum machine.

There are the people who say how brave you are just for being in a wheelchair... "There but for the grace of God" and all that stuff... it's all nonsense... just patronising rubbish. (John Kerrison)

John has found that some people will gravitate to "the guy in the wheelchair" whilst others ignore him as if his wheelchair has somehow magically conferred upon him the ability to become invisible; the latter example angers John the most, he hates to feel excluded. The "does he take sugar?" syndrome is another reaction that disabled people often experience; a situation whereby normally well mannered individuals find themselves unable to communicate directly with someone in a wheelchair. If he encounters any examples of such ignorant behaviour John predictably reacts with loud profanity.

People ask me what it is like to live like this... I use the word "prison" because it feels like I have been a prisoner for more than forty years... I've got this lump of metal stuck around me... I can't be totally spontaneous like I was before. (John Kerrison)

Part VIII - Drumming Again

Chapter Twenty - Three

After the accident I didn't carry on playing the drums with just sticks, without the bass... I didn't do it because I couldn't play the way that I used to play. It wasn't good enough, it wasn't me... I wasn't me anymore. (John Kerrison)

Roughly two years after the accident, while John was still living at his parents' house, he started to look around for ways to return to playing music simply as a way to relieve the boredom. He had made a decision that he would not attempt to play the drums again now that he had lost the use of his legs. In any event he had sold most of his drum kit, the Ludwig 400 snare drum being the only major component that he had retained. John probably kept the snare drum purely for sentimental reasons, after all it was the same model of drum used by one of his hero drummers Joe Morello and his friend Keith Moon had played it. The drum brought back memories of his days as a Rock & Roll drummer which had been savagely curtailed by a freak accident.

John purchased a large xylophone but, perhaps showing a lack of commitment, it was not equipped with any of the electronics required to play at a gig. His choice of musical instrument was based upon the fact that there were no foot pedals and, switching from drumsticks to the small mallets used to strike the xylophones' bars, he could employ the percussion skills that he had acquired as a drummer. It was actually more of a distraction, a way of combatting the boredom, rather than a serious goal of learning to play another instrument. John practised without any of the total commitment he had shown as a small boy learning to play the drums, in the days when he was determined to become a successful drummer. He soon lost all interest in the xylophone and he sold it to buy a small electric organ.

Very conveniently the modestly sized Hammond organ had a "sustain" hand operated switch which could be used instead of a foot pedal. John had gained a good understanding of musical notation as a drummer and hoped that he could apply his acquired skills to playing the keyboard. After many years in the music business he knew plenty of professional keyboard players but, instead of seeking such expert tuition, he made a half hearted attempt to teach himself. John hated being seen in his wheelchair and, having in the past earned a living as a professional musician, he was even more self-conscious about anybody witnessing his less than competent attempts to play the organ; after a short time he again gave up. He put aside all thoughts about being a musician and returned to a sullen withdrawn existence with no constructive thoughts as to his future.

Jean Hall was the chief occupational therapist at Hillingdon Council and she put a great deal of time and effort into helping John. She realised that whilst the physical problems associated with his spinal injury could be partially resolved by adaptations to his parents' house his mental anguish was a much bigger issue. The accident had left a void in John's life, a major part of which was the loss of his ambition to be a drummer. Around 1973 Jean contacted the Hillingdon Young Orchestra and arranged for John to have an audition, his father drove him to the orchestra's rehearsal rooms in Ruislip. The bandleader was a very nice guy, he set up a snare drum with some sheet music. John played very competently but although the orchestra's percussion teacher invited him to return for another session he never went back.

It did not feel right... I wasn't really me. I could read the music and I played really well but I did not want to be looking like a "spaz" in public... I wanted to be a flash bastard like I used to be before the accident. (John Kerrison)

A few years later John got his father to drive him to a music shop in Uxbridge, situated opposite the RAF base, which was run by a professional drummer and saxophonist called Jack Dawkes. For some reason John bought a good quality Pearl Jupiter snare drum without really knowing the reason why. If he had wanted a drum to play he always had his top of the range Ludwig 400 snare drum stashed away at home; however, he probably felt that it was too precious to be used. He messed about with the new drum for a while but eventually he put it away with the rest of what remained of his redundant drumming equipment where it stayed unused for several years.

Whilst he was living at Goshawk Gardens, sometime around the mid 1980s, John was contacted by Sheila Dimmock; the former vocalist and keyboard player in Episode Six. She also put him in touch with Ian Gillan who subsequently paid John a visit and they spent several hours together, reminiscing about the old days. It was the first time that Ian had seen John sitting in a wheelchair but he made no comment about it. John accepted Ian's invitation to spend the day at a recording studio in Barnes where the Rock star was using his instantly recognisable voice on some over dubs. Many years had passed since John had been inside a recording studio and he was fascinated by the huge advances which had been made in new technology.

I was speaking to Ian Gillan backstage after he did a Deep Purple gig in Australia. He said that I was the only drummer in the early sixties that he knew who played "eights on the floor"... that's eight semiquavers played on the bass drum with the foot pedal. Carlo Little used to do it and I kind of nicked it off him. (John Kerrison)

Sheila later hosted a reunion party for former band members of Episode Six at her house in Iver Buckinghamshire; she had by now retired from the music business and was working as a milliner. Her guests included Ian Gillan and Roger Glover who had achieved stardom with the legendary Rock band Deep Purple. Gloria Bristow, who had managed Episode Six, was there with her husband. Tony Barham, a former guitarist in the band, was also present. He was now playing as a semi-professional musician in a social club band whilst working fitting out business premises such as dental surgeries. There was also a celebrity guest at the party called Keith Skues, he was one of the first BBC Radio One disc jockeys. Graham Carter Dimmock and Micky Underwood both failed to make an appearance, the drummer had apparently fallen out with Ian Gillan. John got very drunk whilst everyone swapped anecdotes about their experiences on tour with the band, the atmosphere was very light-hearted with no animosity shown whatsoever concerning their past differences. Afterwards John gave serious consideration to returning to the music business, he wanted to participate in some way, but he could not think of how it could be possible.

You can't play real kick-ass Rock & Roll without a bass drum. The bass drum has been around since at least the 1920s when it was just used to play the pulse of the beat... In the 50s and 60s the bass became a much more integral part of the rhythm context... A lot of the early Rock & Roll drummers didn't play with a syncopated bass drum, it started with drummers playing in Soul bands like the guys backing James Brown. (John Kerrison)

John visited a music shop in Cowley Road Uxbridge just out of interest, to look at the instruments and take the opportunity to mix with musicians, he had no intention of buying anything. Quite by chance the people in the shop were discussing an electronic sample machine that could play the sound of a bass drum. There had been such equipment in the past but the early versions only produced an electronic approximation of a drum sound, the new technology employed digital sampling which gave a much more realistic noise. A company called "Digisound" made a model which cost about £100 and John bought one just to experiment with it, he had no real plans of returning to being a drummer at that time. The book sized box of electronics had a built in amplifier and a small speaker. It was programmed to produce just one sampled sound, the sound of a bass drum for example, when triggered by an electronic switch. It was all quite primitive compared to today's sample programs whereby millions of different individual and composite sounds can be obtained from a basic laptop computer.

The usual method of operating the sound sampler was to attach it to a drum pad or a foot switch but neither option would be of any use to John as it would not enable him to play the rest of a drum kit. He

198

gave the matter a great deal of thought but he could not come up with a practical solution. Trevor Well's mother lived near John's house and his uncle Les often visited her. On one occasion he popped in to see John and they discussed the Digisound box. Les was a retired boffin and he offered to design a switch which John could operate with his mouth.

Early attempts centred on using a switch which was operated by biting it between the teeth but, because it stimulated an excessive amount of saliva in the mouth, it proved to be impractical; furthermore, moisture and electronics rarely go well together. Subsequently Les designed and built a switch, which was operated by air pressure, whereby blowing down a rubber tube inflated a condom which in turn electronically operated the sound sampler. It was a very Heath Robinson affair but it worked rather well. All John had to do was make a "tuh" noise down the tube and the Digisound box produced a corresponding bass drum sound. The mouthpiece was held close to his mouth by attaching it to the microphone arm on a Shure headset. These days John uses a lightweight computer headset with a metal bracket replacing the microphone to hold the blow switch.

The success of the pressure switch encouraged John to try and play the drums again. He put together a drum kit using the Pearl Jupiter snare drum, that he had bought from Jack Dawkes music shop some years earlier, and he purchased three tom-toms plus some peripheral hardware. The tom-toms were made by a company called "Diamond" which were imported from China by a company called Percussion Services Ltd run by one of John's friends called Roy Webster; there was no need for a bass drum because that role was replaced by the Digisound sampler. Despite being inexpensive the new drums had reasonable quality heads, the most important feature of any drum. John bought them instead of an expensive professional kit mostly for financial reasons and perhaps partly because he wasn't totally confident about drumming again. Having the top of the range equipment can be very embarrassing if you haven't really learned to master it. "All the gear and no idea", as they say.

I was worried that I would not be able to play like I used to. When I was young I never looked at it that way because I was an arrogant little git… after the accident, when I started again, I was a little bit apprehensive. (John Kerrison)

John had been taught to play the drums by the legendary Jim Marshall and, throughout his career prior to the accident, he had set up his drum kit pretty much in the same conventional way that his venerable tutor had instructed him. A drummer would usually sit with their legs either side of the snare drum which put the bass drum pedal within reach. The snare would normally be tilted, pointing way from the seated drummer, enabling standard drumming techniques such as the "rim-shot". This involves producing an accentuated back beat by striking the drum head with the tip of the drumstick whilst simultaneously hitting the shaft of the drum stick against the rim of the drum. The sound created in this manner can be varied according to the distance from the rim that the drum head is played. Such "overtones" are used in a wide variety of musical genres and, although Jazz drummer Gene Kruper is often credited with developing the rim-shot, the technique probably originated in military marching bands.

Whilst John had no need to reach a bass drum pedal the wheel chair prevented him from placing his legs around the snare drum; tilting the drum head away from himself put it even further out of his reach. In the standard set up he could not get close enough to the snare drum in order to comfortably play the rim-shot and the other variations of the drumming technique. After much trial and error John ended up tilting the snare drum towards himself, so that it was now within his reach, but this produced another major problem: he found it nearly impossible to drum whilst holding the drum sticks in the same way that he had always done.

Prior to the accident he had employed what is known as the "traditional" grip which involves holding a drumstick in the left hand between the arch of the thumb and then through two fingers, playing the snare drum with the palm of the hand facing upwards. The grip on the drumstick in the right hand is quite different, the shaft is held between the thumb and first finger whilst using the other fingers to control it. John found that he now had to fundamentally alter the way that he held the drum sticks and changed over to using the "matched" grip. In this style the drumsticks are held the same way in both hands. The drumstick is held by the first finger with the index finger curled around the shaft and secured by placing the thumb on top. This allows for a certain amount of controlled bounce when the drum head is struck.

These days John favours the "Vinnie Colaiuta" drumstick which was designed by the famously versatile drummer and manufactured by Zildjian. They are very near to being a chunky "5B", a size commonly used by Heavy Rock drummers, but not quite the same. Drum sticks are conventionally numbered according to their weight, length, diameter, shape and tip construction. Number "5" sticks are like knitting needles and "N" denotes a nylon tip. However, the numbering system varies amongst the different manufacturers and the end result is quite bewildering even to most professional drummers.

Sometimes you can recognise a drummer just from his style and sometimes you can't... but you can always tell if he can "dance". (John Kerrison)

John found that he still knew how to play the drums, the technique and the music, plus there was still a great deal of "muscle memory" remaining in his hands and his arms even after such a long passage of time. Nevertheless, he realised that it would take a great deal of practise to fully regain his pre-accident skills. Furthermore, he would have to find a way of integrating the Digisound sampler with his newly acquired drumming style imposed by his disability. There were no books or training courses available on the subject and John had to go back to basics, working it all out for himself. Slowly but surely the obsession with drumming that first began when he was a teenage schoolboy started to return.

Before the accident I was always quite skinny... using my arms to propel the wheelchair has really built up my shoulders and biceps. (John Kerrison)

Learning to play the drums again in such an unusual format proved to be quite a challenge.

On a visit to Uxbridge John met up with his friend Roger Willis and enlisted his support plus his technical expertise. Roger was a mobility instructor, working with children who have a visual impairment, a vocation requiring unlimited patience and dedication. However, in the 1970s he had played the drums with the chart topping pop band "Christie" and also with the Prog Rock band "Capability Brown". John went to his house every Wednesday where together they practised playing the drums with the Digisound sampler. With Roger's invaluable assistance John was soon making great progress.

Everyone has their own stuff and their own style... I can do stuff that some other drummers can't do and likewise some drummers can do stuff that I can't do. (John Kerrison)

Drummers usually hire specially sound proofed rehearsal rooms in order to hone their skills without forcing their neighbours to seek court orders concerning the antisocial noise levels. An alternative is to use practise pads which do not make anywhere near as much noise as the real thing; professional percussionists sometimes also use them to warm up backstage prior to a big concert. The pads are usually manufactured from the same material as the real thing to replicate the same feel and reaction when drumming but with a much reduced volume of sound; they can be placed on top of the drums in a real drum kit or set up on a frame. Roger had a set of drum pads made by "Bill Saunders" which he and John used in their Wednesday night practise sessions.

Drummers are naturally very competitive, they all want to show off... in some ways it becomes less competitive as you get older. (John Kerrison)

John and Roger worked together as they fathomed how to use the practice drums alongside the Digisound sampler. They used half of the drum pad kit each and took turns without using the drum sampler, they just mouthed the "tuh... tuh... tuh...." noises required to trigger the sound machine. Whilst playing together they constantly showed off their acquired skills, trying to outdo one another, performing subtle grace notes, strokes, diddles, drags, flams, rolls and so on. Their joint success really encouraged John and he started to become more confident that he could actually become quite competent using the digisound machine. However, he still found the whole thing very odd; he didn't actually like playing that way but it was the only way that he could get back to being a Rock & Roll drummer.

Rock & Roll drummers don't usually play adhering precisely to a score like a percussion player in an orchestra would have to. (John Kerrison)

Between them the two drummers owned plenty of books detailing the various drumming patterns which had been created by top drummers such as Melvin Parker and Clyde Stubblefield. One book they referred to most was called "The Drummer's Cookbook"; they went through it from cover to cover practising the drumming patterns whilst learning how to best employ the Digisound sampler. Drum notation often employs a simplified form of written music which is designed for ease of use and not, as often suggested in the myriad number of drummer jokes, because percussion players are mentally impaired.

Drum notation is set out so as not to confuse anyone... especially seeing as how drummers are a lot of easily confused people. (John Kerrison)

With a lot of hard work and Roger's invaluable assistance John eventually regained his former drumming skills. In addition, and perhaps more importantly, he also recovered an important part of his life from which he had been separated for so many unbearably long years. No longer just "a thing in a wheelchair" he was now a drummer again, his sense of self worth was slowly restored.

One day Roger said to me 'We must get you a really good gig"... We played together at a place somewhere in Slough... it was at a New Year's Eve party. It was my first gig for nearly two decades since the accident. (John Kerrison)

Part IX - Gigging Again

Chapter Twenty - Four

I got a phone call from a guy called Martin who asked me "We need a drummer, do you play with balls?" to which I replied "I'll come down and you can hear me"... I had to explain about the wheelchair after I got there. (John Kerrison)

It happened the same way that it always used to happen, just like back in the sixties. A band needed a drummer and somebody, probably someone in a West London music shop, recommended John Kerrison. However, it was now 1988 and John had not played as a professional musician since his accident around seventeen years earlier. The audition was for a Rhythm & Blues revival act who mimicked the stage performances of "The Blues Brothers' Show Band and Revue" as seen in the 1980 film "The Blues Brothers". It was a very popular format copied by several bands playing in pubs and clubs during the late 1980s. John had practised hard learning to play the drums again, integrating the bass drum sound sampler into his technique, but he had rarely performed in public since his accident.

I used to go and see my mate Nick Simper when he was in a band called "Flying Fox" which Frankie Reid had set up before he went to Australia... subsequently the band became "The Good Old Boys". Sometimes they used to get me up to do a bit on the drums if they could get me there, in my wheelchair, behind the drum kit. (John Kerrison)

When John set up his kit there was almost certainly some initial apprehension amongst the Blues Brothers tribute band who, before he turned up for the audition, had not realised that he did not have the use of his legs. Furthermore, the lack of a bass drum and the strange electronic sampler triggered by a blow switch was not the normal set-up to which they were accustomed. However, when they heard John demonstrate his drumming ability they soon discovered that he did in fact play with plenty of "balls" and he was readily accepted into the line-up.

The band had a constantly fluctuating membership of semi-professional musicians from all around West London and beyond. Only the two front men dressed up as the character roles of Joliet Jake and his brother Elwood from the movie. The pair of lead vocalists both wore the black suits plus black neckties with white shirts and pork pie hats, copying the costumes in the film, but the performance was more about serious Blues and Soul music than a comedy act. The blow switch designed by Les and the digital bass sound machine worked extremely well without any major glitches. John felt none of the trepidation associated with stage fright when he began performing in public again after so many years absence from the lime light. His old arrogance returned and he was superbly confident about his ability as a drummer.

John was living in Hayes at that time and he drove himself to and from the gigs in a Ford Cortina Estate fitted with hand controls. Transporting the drum kit was made much easier by the absence of a large and cumbersome bass drum, the digital sampler took up much less space. He often gave a lift to fellow band member Neil Cowley and he soon realised that the fifteen year old keyboard player was a musical genius. Whilst Neil was very young to be playing with a band it should be noted that John was himself only thirteen when he began playing as a professional musician. However, Neil lacked the arrogant self confidence that John exhibited at his age and asked him if he thought that he would achieve success in the music business. John assured the young concert level pianist that he would most definitely make it right to the top. Neil later went on to become a very successful Jazz musician, playing with his own band, and he has also played on several recordings by internationally famous performers including "Adele" and "The Stereophonics".

The band played mostly in small venues such as pubs and clubs where the blow trigger, because it worked so well, hardly attracted any attention. Sometimes someone in the audience would be curious as to how a guy in a wheelchair could play the drums but, once the gig had started, it barely got noticed when the band was playing. After about eight or nine months, perhaps feeling that the Blues Brothers act had run its course, the band leader Martin and his wife enrolled John and Neil into a four piece social club band. John played with the "spin off" group for a while until he was asked to put in money towards the purchase of a new PA amplifier system. He had purchased his own kit without assistance and could not see why he should have to contribute towards the cost of the rest of the gear; it was the same situation which caused his departure from Paul and the Alpines in 1963.

Shortly after departing from the band John received a telephone call from a man called Keith Adamson, as usual the recommendation had come about by word of mouth. Keith was a semi-professional musician who played both guitar and keyboards. He had set up a social club band of his own and he had plenty of gigs booked but he was short of a drummer and asked John to help him out. The four piece band performed at quite a few of the working mens' clubs around Hayes, Feltham and Kingston. Their play list consisted of covers of present day hits and vintage numbers from the sixties, John knew many of the earlier songs because had played them when they were first released. The band folded after less than a year when Keith decided that he would try to achieve success as a composer, concentrating his talents on writing scores for films and television dramas.

The next band to appear on John's extensive curriculum vitae was called "Hot Jelly Roll". John was recruited by Don Rice who fronted the band and played the harmonica in addition to being the lead singer. Hot Jelly Roll were a four piece band and, as can be guessed from the name, they were very much dedicated to the Blues genre. John played with the band for about a year until he had a fall out with Don. Hot Jelly Roll searched for a new drummer and, giving a sense of history repeating itself, they recruited none other than John's old friend Mick Underwood who had taken over from him when he got sacked from The Episode. Their paths had crossed several time since the days when they were both tutored by Jim Marshall. Around that time John had another blast from his past when Frankie Reid returned to West London on a visit from his home in Australia. John had played in Frankie's band "Frankie Reid and the Casuals" in the mid 1960s before the singer moved to Perth. The pair of old friends played together in a nostalgic reunion gig at the Rising Sun public house in Sudbury. John also occasionally deputised for the drummer in The Good Old Boys alongside Nick Simper on bass guitar, Alan Barratt on lead vocals, Pete Parks on lead guitar and Simon Bishop on rhythm.

Shortly after John moved to Shepperton in 1997 he got another call from Keith Adamson who asked him to help set up a function band. They recruited some other musicians and held rehearsal sessions in a Feltham studio. The line-up consisted of a female vocalist called Heidi McCafferty and a lead guitar player called Colin Charles.

Colin Charles was in an early sixties group called "The 4" which played at many of the seaside holiday camps in that era... They had a single called "It's Alright" which was released in 1964 on the Decca label. (John Kerrison)

The band still didn't have a name or any bookings when Keith Adamson left to pursue other interests. He was replaced by Barry Parfitt on keyboards and the band adopted the name "High Life". Early on Norman Mitchener, John's friend from "The Beachcombers", joined the band and his twelve year old son Tom Mitchener played the saxophone. Afterwards the band's line-up constantly fluctuated.

There was a succession of bass guitarists. Steve Hargreaves was replaced by bass guitarist Mark Milner, followed by two more bass players... and then there was quite a quite flashy guy called Keith who drove a Ferrari and had a flat in California... eventually the band settled down with Paul Myerson. (John Kerrison)

The Chinese manufactured Diamond tom-toms were still giving John good service but he decided that it was time to update the Digisound box and the blow trigger which Les had designed. He purchased an Alesis D4 drum module, advances in new technology meant that it had the capacity for far more sounds than the Digisound was capable of producing. John contacted a company in Aylesbury called "Possum" who made suck and blow switches that enable quadriplegic people to control and steer an electric wheelchair. He drove to their Buckinghamshire factory and bought one of their technologically advanced control units. John then got in touch with an electrical engineer called Steve Hargreaves, a former bass guitarist in Frankie Reid & the Casuals, and got him to modify the switch so that it could be used to operate the Alesis D4 drum module. The final ensemble worked extremely well.

John experimented with a different set-up to his drum kit when he purchased some new "Flats" tom-toms made by Arbiter. They were like standard drums but comprised just a drum head with no shells. The unorthodox design had the advantage of being lightweight and took up very little room when transported, compared to normal sized drums; an important feature when there is also a wheelchair to get into the car. However, John did not like the sound quality of the Flats tom-toms and he soon got rid of them, reverting back to using his more conventional drum kit format again. Drummers often own several drums and John is no exception, he has amassed quite a large and extensive collection over the years.

I bought a beautiful wooden snare drum which was made by my mate Gary Noonan. I bought it just because I liked it. It is made from turned and polished solid Brazilian mahogany hardwood... it shows the grain. To me it represents the beauty of woodworking and drumming altogether in one. (John Kerrison)

High Life benefitted from having a good agent who got them work at several top venues and corporate events; the quality of their performances earned them many repeat bookings. The function band dressed in smart dinner jackets, formal attire being essential when performing at upmarket establishments such as the Grosvenor, the Hilton, the Café de Paris and the Dorchester. John had played at several of the prestigious venues prior to the accident, when he was drumming with The Beachcombers.

The function band had a large repertoire of songs but even so they sometimes had to "wing it" when required. On one occasion they were booked to play at a corporate event on a large boat which cruised up and down the River Thames. It was supposed to be themed as a James Bond night and there were clips from the Bond films, lots of large still photographs and plenty of Bond paraphernalia. The band repeatedly played the well known James Bond "signature" theme tune music over and over again in between their usual numbers, mainly because they didn't have any other James Bond movie tracks in their repertoire. Nevertheless they still managed to pull it off and they gave a very praiseworthy performance.

John was using the Alesis D4 digital sampler plugged into a Trace Elliot speaker, which he had bought second hand, but he was not happy with the bass drum sound; the speaker didn't seem to have the required bottom frequencies. John replaced the speaker with a pair of JBL Eon 15 speakers, they had a very high technical specification but the sound that they produced was still a little too "sweet" for his ear. Overall the performance of the electronic replacement for the bass drum was quite good but it could never be perfect. A problem with digitally sampled drums is that, unless triggered by something sensitive like a drum pad, it is not possible to produce a dynamic and responsive drum sound. When operated with a straightforward switch the sampler will only will give out the sound which has been sampled, there is very little variation available apart from the usual volume and tone controls on the amplifier.

I had a Trace Elliot speaker that I wasn't using and Eddie Richards said that his keyboard player could do with it. I told him he could take it away and pay me a hundred quid for it later... but he never did. That was about 15 years ago and I haven't seen him since. (John Kerrison)

On the night of 31 December 1999 John missed out on the chance to see in the new millennium playing with High Life, at a big corporate gig, because he was in bed with a viral infection. However, he soon recovered and returned to gigging with the band. Things went well with High Life for another couple of years until they performed at a Christmas party in Tilbury in 2001. The agreed fee for the evening was quite generous and John was looking forward to a very good Yuletide payday. However, the money was paid by cheque to the band's lead singer who, citing problems with their bank account, failed to hand over any cash to the rest of the band until months later. It was a situation which John found unacceptable and, when he eventually got paid, he quit the band. Barry Parfitt also voiced his disapproval concerning the late payment and he departed from the High Life line-up shortly afterwards.

By this time John decided that he needed a top quality professional drum kit and he got rid of his serviceable, but less than boast worthy, Chinese made tom-toms. He commissioned the fabrication of a complete new set of drums which were made by his friend Gary Noonan of "Noonan Custom Drums" in Gravesend Kent. The drum shells were wrapped in a pink sparkle finish and equipped with Gary's own top quality fittings. John had not bought a bass drum for the Chinese kit but this time he had a matching pink sparkle bass drum made for cosmetic reasons only. The first time that John played the new drums was in a recording studio and he was very impressed by the sound. The RIMS suspension mounts, designed not to interfere with resonance, made the drums "sing". It was a drum kit which any professional drummer would be proud to own.

Whilst John had been playing with High Life he often crossed paths with a group who were called "Gold". The band members were mostly from Hayes and included George Williams and Mick Baker who John had known for many years; there was also a female vocalist and a saxophone player. When Barry Parfitt and John joined the band they signed up with an agent who already had a group on his books called Gold and so they changed the name to "Red Wind". The new name was chosen because the bass player had previously been in a band called Red Wind.

The Possum trigger switch had worked well for several years but eventually it began to malfunction. John sought the assistance of an organisation called REMAP who he had heard about through his friend Trevor Wells. REMAP are a charitable group who were founded in the mid 1960s; they design and build customised pieces of equipment for disabled people. Their volunteer members are mostly retired engineers and wonderfully "nutty professor" types, eccentrics who enjoy utilising their expert skills in engineering and electronics to solve problems for which no there is no commercially available product.

They built a modified easel for Trevor so that, despite his quadriplegia, he is able to paint to a very high standard. The one-off bespoke item is typical of the work that they undertake without charging a fee for their services. REMAP examined John's requirements and tailor made a blow switch for him. They continue to keep him in business as a drummer and his current trigger was made by a REMAP member called Brian Tilbury. Whilst John is grateful for the assistance provided by REMAP he is nevertheless rather disappointed that his blow trigger is not one of the case histories detailed on their website.

I was interviewed on BBC Radio 4 when they did a programme about the work done by REMAP. They recorded me playing the drums in my house at Hillingdon... it was on the Internet for a while. (John Kerrison)

John had been using the Alesis D4 drum sampler for several years and he decided that it was time to buy a new machine. He chose a Roland TD-10 electronic drum machine because, at that time, it was at the cutting edge of new technology; furthermore it was entirely compatible for use with the trigger designed by REMAP. The new drum module came with a hefty price tag of about two thousand pounds but John got one at a discount price through a friend in the business. However, he still had to drive all the way to Birmingham to pick it up. In no time at all John mastered the new drum module and found that it represented a marked improvement in both sound quality and versatility.

The band went to a recording studio in order to make a promotional CD, to get more bookings, but John was not at all happy with the poor quality of the final product. He took the music files to Tom Mitchener, who had his own studio in Oxhey near Watford, and asked him if he could do anything with them. Tom remastered the recordings and they sounded a whole lot better. The band were reasonably successful but after a while the saxophone player and the female vocalist quit; subsequently John fell out with George and also left the band. At that time John was already involved in another project, he joined forces with a musician by the name of Adrian Connery. Together with Nick Simper and Pete Parks from the Good Old Boys plus Barry Parfitt, they set up a Country Rock band called "Blagards & Cowboys".

Part X - Blagards & Cowboys

Chapter Twenty - Five

Even after all these years I still don't feel that I have beaten it… it never goes away… there is a lack of any spontaneity in my life because everything has to be planned, even simple stuff… The only positive side is that I have gained some great friends. (John Kerrison)

In 2007 John was at a football match watching his team Hayes FC play at home when, quite by chance, he bumped into a guitarist called Alan Dove. They had first met many years beforehand in the early 1960s when Alan was just seven or eight years old. At that time his middle brother Dave Dove was the bass guitarist playing in a band with John called "Paul and the Alpines". Alan had been touring around Norway in a duo and he spoke very enthusiastically about his fellow musician who was called Adrian Connery. That evening John held a barbecue at his house in Hillingdon and Alan brought Adrian along to meet him.

I was drinking with my cousin at the barbecue when Adrian Connery turned up with his son Damian who was about fifteen at that time. When it got late Damian told his father that he wanted to go home but Adrian told him he was talking to a very important person so he would just have to wait. (John Kerrison)

Adrian lives in Devon and though he had not met John before going to the barbecue he had seen him play when Red Wind performed in a gig at Exeter University. Furthermore, Adrian originally hailed from the same area as John and as a boy he attended the Botwell Junior School in Hayes town. One of his music teachers was Father Phil from the Immaculate Heart of Mary Roman Catholic Church in Hayes; coincidentally Father Phil was the same priest who organised the trips that John went on to Lourdes. In the 1970s, when he was still a teenager at school, Adrian played in several different bands performing around the London pub circuit. Later he went on to work in Jersey and the Canaries followed by tours of Scandinavia, the USA and Europe. He is a very talented musician, so much so that at a recent gig a lady told him that he should be on a very popular television talent show which she mistakenly referred to as "The X Files".

I don't do a lot of writing myself... I try to when I'm in the mood... Usually I add to the interpretation by suggesting a word here and there or even a line... In a couple of the songs I wrote a lot more of the words. (John Kerrison)

On a subsequent visit Adrian stayed for a week at John's house, travelling up from his seaside home in the West Country with his guitar and keyboard. Adrian played several of the songs that he had composed and John was very impressed. They collaborated together reworking some of the tunes, the arrangements and writing additional material; the overall style falling mainly in the "Rock Country" musical genre. Rather than waste their efforts they decided to form a band and record an album. John got in touch with Tom Mitchener at his recording studio in Oxhey near Watford and booked some recording sessions. With John playing the drums and Adrian on lead vocals plus guitar all that was needed was some additional musicians.

John's good friend Nick Simper, who he had played alongside in "The Pirates", readily agreed to join the band; the former Deep Purple bass guitarist added a great deal of Hard Rock credibility and prestige to the project. Lead guitarist Peter Parks was also a valuable recruit; he had performed with Nick in the Heavy Rock band "Warhorse" and also with B.B.King, Paul McCartney, Simple Minds plus Nick's current band "The Good Old Boys". The line-up was enhanced by gifted keyboard player Barry Parfitt; his first recording with the Prog Rock band "Walrus" in 1970 is now a highly sought after collector's item. Barry has played in a variety of bands encompassing a wide range of musical styles including the jazz-oriented outfit "Special Edition". Roger Willis was also an extremely useful addition to the band; formerly a drummer with groups such as Christie and Capability Brown, he provided vocal harmonies and helped write some of the arrangements.

It was Adrian who came up with the name "Blagards & Cowboys" for the new band, he was very much inspired by fact that both John and Nick had played in The Pirates. Following a similar theme the album was given the title of "Skulduggery". It took quite a long time to complete the album, matching studio bookings with the availability of all those involved was always going to be a logistical challenge. In the recording studio John would listen to a metronomic "click" sound played through headphones whilst he laid down the drum track for a song, assisted by a "guide" melody of vocals and guitar supplied by Adrian. The vocals, guitars and keyboard elements were then added in layers to produce the finished song.

The Blagards & Cowboys album "Skulduggery" was published with nine of the songs which John and Adrian had worked on together and a tenth track which was a cover version of a Country & Western "standard".

Track 1 - Inside Out Again. The lyrics describe the jealousy sometimes shown by family and so called "good friends".

I'm inside out again, I don't know where I've been
I met myself again, I'm inside out again
This time I'm going to make amends
I'll see you down the road my friend...
...singing Country songs, and I will survive.
(Copyright © Connery and Kerrison - reproduced by kind permission)

Track 2 - Too Close for Comfort. Musicians who have settled down still feel that restless desire to be back on the road again with a band.

I'm too close for comfort, too close to the fire
Too much of a drifter, wanting to get higher
That gypsy blooded man you love was hurting deep inside

215

He'd been missing out on everything, missing out on life

Track 3 - Northern Girl. The wonderfully moving lyrics actually refer to a young woman that Adrian met in Norway. Nevertheless, the sentiments expressed in the song appear to have equal relevance to John's deep depression following the accident and the breakdown of his marriage to a lady from the North England town of Salford.

I was blind but now I see
Deep down inside of me
There's a memory of a girl that lingers on
Now the nights are getting long
And the time since she was gone
Is just a cold and empty misery for me
It's hard to find a way
I just make it through the day
Northern Girl won't you come back to me to stay
Northern Girl

Track 4 - White Horses of Lyme Bay. The initial inspiration for this bouncy "holiday" tune came after Nick Simper fell off some scaffolding and broke his ankle when he was working on a house in Lyme Regis. Later Adrian was sitting on a beach watching the "white horse" waves and that prompted him into writing the lyrics. A sign in the seaside town of Paignton advertising "River Cruises and Steam Trains" provided a line for the chorus.

White horses of Lyme Bay
River cruises and steam trains
White horses of Lyme Bay
On a late September day

Track 5 - Blagards & Cowboys. The song title eventually also gave the band its name, originally written as "Modern Day Cowboys" it was changed to better suit the tune. It is very much in the California-Country-Rock style of "The Eagles", invoking a poignancy somewhat reminiscent of "Desperado".

You Blagards and Cowboys, listen to me
A wondering minstrel's not something to be
Restless outlaws everywhere
Wanted by someone, someone who cares
... don't die with your boots on you Blagards and Cowboys.
(Copyright © Connery and Kerrison - reproduced by kind permission)

Track 6 - No Win Scenario. This is very much a Country & Western song. John went to see his team Hayes FC play at an away match and during the half-time break in an apparently deadlocked game the DJ played No Win Scenario; it was an apt choice in the circumstances.

It's a no-win scenario wondering which way to go
I'm tired of chasing dreams which won't come true
I'm going home to where my love, she waits
This time I will not hesitate
I realise that I've been such a fool
It's a no win scenario with you
(Copyright © Connery and Kerrison - reproduced by kind permission)

Track 7 - Old Habits Die Hard. The downward spiral in the life of a gambler.

I was drumming to the click track and Adrian's melody in my headphones... when it got to the middle eight I knew that it had to go half time... it was in my head... I just knew it. Adrian was signalling to me to keep it going because he liked it. (John Kerrison)

John and Adrian had a great deal of trouble with the song's arrangement until Roger Willis came to their assistance. He also provided additional vocals on the recording.

217

... never turn him face up, put him back in the pack while you
can
The dealer has the edge and he never backs a gambling man
Gambling man, bad habits start young, old habits die hard
Better pick another card, Gambling man
(Copyright © Connery and Kerrison - reproduced by kind
permission)

Track 8 - Angels Falls. This song is about alcohol, the good things and the bad things that come about drinking in a bar. The lyrics were written in a hotel room with just a bottle of Jack Daniels for company.

It ain't Rock and Roll, but the hangover's still the same
Where he sits now there ain't no one else that he can blame
Luck took him down from high ground once again
He's alone in the desert, alone with no friends
It ain't Rock and Roll but the hangover's still the same
No, it ain't Rock and Roll but the hangover's still the same
(Copyright © Connery and Kerrison - reproduced by kind
permission)

Track 9 - I'm Always Waiting for Her. Tongue-in-cheek lyrics about the perennial cliché concerning women. John and Adrian also wrote another arrangement for this song with a "Cajun" style.

I'm always waiting for her, I know
It doesn't matter which way we go
Sometimes it's trouble and strife
I'm going to make her my wife
I'm always waiting for her
(Copyright © Connery and Kerrison - reproduced by kind
permission)

Track 10 - Six Days on the Road. Written by Earl Green and Carl Montgomery this classic Country & Western song is something of a "standard" in the music business and it has been recorded by several performers; in particular it was a hit for "Taj Mahal" in the late 1960s. John recalls that, due to the proficiency of the musicians

218

involved, it took the Blagards & Cowboys less than half an hour to finish recording the "truck driving" track in the studio.

The Skulduggery album received excellent reviews in the Country & Western music press. Maverick Magazine gave the album four and a half stars with similar praise awarded by Southern Country Magazine, FATEA Magazine and Cross Country magazine. Tracks from the Skulduggery album have been given air time on Country & Western radio station programmes in the UK, USA and several other countries around the world. A certain amount of interest concerning "White Horses of Lyme Bay" was shown in Tasmania which has its own "Lime" Bay coastal feature. The song also achieved a number five spot on the British and Irish Country Hot Disc Chart and was voted to the number one position on the UK Country Song Writers' Chart. In addition "White Horses of Lyme Bay" was chosen as one of the tracks for the compilation album "Best of British & Irish Country 2011" (released on the Xiaohua label - XIA 1).

The Blagards & Cowboys album Skulduggery can be purchased through Amazon, iTunes and Purple Records. Further details concerning the band and their current music catalogue can be found on their website www.blagardsandcowboys.com.

Even the most modest of the album's Internet sales are celebrated by Adrian. He reported the purchase of a track from Skulduggery by a Country Rock fan in Tokyo with the somewhat hyperbolical announcement "We've broken into the Japanese market".

John is now a pensioner and as he approaches seventy he remains very active. Currently he is writing more songs with Adrian for a new album. One of the Blagards & Cowboys' recently recorded Country Rock songs called "Still" is particularly impressive.

When it suits you, you will pass me on the street
And other times you'll turn and walk away
Then with indifference you'll creep right up on me
With baited breath I wait to hear the words I know you'll say
Are you still?
Yeah, I'm having a good time losing,
Are you still?
Yes, I'm having a ball getting it wrong

I'm bad, I'm bad all inclusive
Can't take it with me when I'm gone
(Copyright © Connery and Kerrison - reproduced by kind
permission)

The lyrics of Still are very appropriate. John "Still" has the same obsession with drumming that began as a schoolboy, back in those times when he made a snare drum from a biscuit tin and a piece of wallpaper.

I went to the West Country to visit Adrian and he introduced me to a guy called Robin Hill. He had just written a novel based upon the tracks in the Skulduggery album and called it "Blagards & Cowboys". Over a couple of beers I told him a few anecdotes about my life and he said that someone should write a book about me... I said OK, let's do it. (John Kerrison)

More than seventy separate interviews followed that initial meeting with John and his recollections were accumulated into a biography chronicling his life. Sometimes it was a painful process for him as he recounted several distressing incidents in his life with self-deprecating honesty, often commenting that it was a cathartic experience. However, there was still a fair amount of humour even when he was detailing the most desperate of those dark episodes. Over a period of ten months John recalled the best and the worst of what he had achieved; disclosing details of actions for which he was still ashamed, boasting of proud moments, joking about amusing experiences and reminiscing from wonderful memories concerning his family, friends and fellow musicians... both those still living and the many who are now long departed. John has outlived most of the musicians that he hung around with in Jim Marshall's music shop when he was still at school. However, many of their names live on as legends in Rock & Roll.

I know that there's no "closure" with my loss, the feeling of bereavement is always there. For me it has never become "normal"... I'm reminded about the whole thing every time that I wake up. (John Kerrison)

Blagards & Cowboys have recently returned to Tom Mitchener's recording studio to make a new album which has currently been assigned the working title of "Still". At the end of one demo click track featuring John's drumming his cheeky West London voice can be heard asking "Was that all right?".

Readers can visit _www.blagardsandcowboys.com_ and decide for themselves.

In Loving Memory

Trevor Wells
1 November 1956 - 13 September 2015

Shortly after the completion of this biography Trevor Wells passed away at Stoke Mandeville Hospital following a respiratory infection. Whilst playing rugby in 1978 he sustained a severe neck injury. Despite the subsequent near total paralysis Trevor went on to become a most respected professional artist and a prominent member of the Mouth and Foot Painting Artists.

Trevor was a truly remarkable man and a very close friend. I will miss those happy times that I spent together with him and his wonderful wife Shirley... precious memories that will stay with me forever. Always a courageous fighter and an inspiration to all, he leaves behind a superb legacy in the beautiful artwork that he so skilfully created. (John Kerrison)

Printed in Great Britain
by Amazon